REFLECTIONS

A Layperson Reads the Bible

Jack Richbourg

CONTENTS

INTRODUCTION

I am a religious hybrid. My mother was raised a Baptist. My father was raised a Methodist. I was raised an Episcopalian only to convert to Unitarian Universalism in my early twenties. I consider myself an atheist, agnostic, humanist, theist, evangelical, born again Christian. I have been all of those things at one time or another and am a conglomeration of them all now.

I have always enjoyed talking about religion with my friends. One friend because of my interest in religion invited me to the Bible Study class at his Episcopal church which happened to be the very church I had attended before my conversion to Unitarian Universalism. I had gone to youth group there and was confirmed in that church so I was no stranger to the place.

The members of this Trinitarian group welcomed me in spite of my Unitarian tendencies, and I became, as I grew to know them, more empowered to talk about the Bible in a Trinitarian venue from a Unitarian point of view. They taught me many things about the Bible that I did not know, and I may have taught them some things they did not know. My Unitarian minister once said to me, "Tell all your Trinitarian friends that we, Unitarians, put a great deal of emphasis on the *third person* of the Trinity," and I have obediently tried to do just that. From my reading of the Bible, I have concluded that Jesus of Nazareth had pre-humanist ideas upon which post-humanism is based. He most certainly recognized the divine spirit within himself and others

After some time in my Bible Study, I began attending the Sunday evening service at my new/old church. My sister went to that church also, and sometimes I would accompany her to the evening service. I loved the service. They did not make me recite a creed. As a Unitarian I am very suspicious of creeds. The service was very contemplative. I loved the quietude and the Taizé chants. I became a regular attendee of this evening Episcopal service. On Sunday mornings, I attended the Unitarian Church, and on Sunday evenings, I went to the Episcopal Church. I think I must be a Unitarian who just likes the sacrament of Holy Communion. Did I mention that I was a religious hybrid?

It was the custom at this service that a lay member of the congregation give a five-to-six-minute reflection on the Gospel lesson assigned that Sunday. After a while, I was asked to give the reflection, and I enjoyed it. I found it to be a very profound spiritual exercise to roll a Gospel reading around in my head until I had some deeper connection to it. Sometimes I would place myself into the story by identifying with one of the characters. This gave me a new perspective. It allowed me to enter into the story, to walk around inside the story and observe things I might have missed otherwise. It became a story about me, right here, right now; rather than a story told about people I never knew, who lived far away, a long time ago. It made scripture relevant. It has proved to me that revelation is not sealed, that there can always be new, more relevant meanings to the old symbols and texts.

I gave these reflections every month or two for several years. Some of them follow, but before you read them, I would like to define a term that I have used in them. To begin with, you should know that I have only a little formal religious training. I learned my catechism as a boy and have listened to some very good sermons over the year. The last two years, I have taken courses at Memphis Theological Seminary, and I have read a lot of books on theology and spirituality. I have been greatly influenced by the writings of John Shelby Spong, Marcus Borg, Brian McLaren, and Richard Rohr. Rohr, in particular, has taught me the meaning of the word, "Christ." This is a word that comes with a lot of baggage. Unitarians for the most part do not like it because they believe it ascribes some sort of divine status to the man, Jesus. To be correct, Christ is the Greek translation for the Hebrew word, "Messiah," which has been translated into English as "the anointed one of God." In a sense, all of us have been anointed by God through our births and ongoing lives. We are a part of a continuously, unfolding creation, and, therefore, are material manifestations of the Spirit that created us. Thus, Rohr defines Christ as the over-arching presence of the Spirit in all things. This "Christ" was there at creation. It was in the man, Jesus. This Spirit is in you and me and is eternally present in all material things. We may not see it. We can be blind to it, but it is there nonetheless, and always has been.

So, with that one definition, you may now read my reflections. I hope there are other religious hybrids like me out there who might enjoy reading them as much as I have enjoyed writing them.

May the words of my mouth and the meditations of my heart be acceptable in your sight, oh Lord, my strength and my redeemer.

THE ROAD TO EMMAUS

N ow on that same day two of Jesus' disciples were going to a village called Emmaus, about seven miles from Jerusalem, and talking with each other about all these things that had happened. While they were talking and discussing, Jesus himself came near and went with them, but their eyes were kept from recognizing him. And he said to them, "What are you discussing with each other while you walk along?" They stood still, looking sad. Then one of them, whose name was Cleopas, answered him, "Are you the only stranger in Jerusalem who does not know the things that have taken place there in these days?" He asked them, "What things?" They replied, "The things about Jesus of Nazareth, who was a prophet mighty in deed and word before God and all the people, and how our chief priests and leaders handed him over to be condemned to death and crucified him. But we had hoped that he was the one to redeem Israel. Yes, and besides all this, it is now the third day since these things took place. Moreover, some women of our group astounded us. They were at the tomb early this morning, and when they did not find his body there, they came back and told us that they had indeed seen a vision of angels who said that he was alive. Some of those who were with us went to the tomb and found it just as the women had said; but they did not see him." Then he said to them, "Oh, how foolish you are, and how slow of heart to believe all that the prophets have declared! Was it not necessary that the Messiah should suffer these things and then enter into his glory?" Then beginning with Moses and all the prophets, he interpreted to them the things about himself in all the scriptures.

As they came near the village to which they were going, he walked ahead as if he were going on. But they urged him strongly, saying, "Stay with us, because it is almost evening and the day is now nearly over." So, he went in to stay with them. When he was at the table with them, he took bread, blessed and broke it, and gave it to them. Then their eyes were opened, and they recognized him; and he vanished from their sight. They said to each other, "Were not our hearts burning within us while he was talking to us on the road, while he was opening the scriptures to us?" That same hour they got up and returned to Jerusalem; and they found the eleven and their companions gathered together. They were saying, "The Lord has risen indeed, and he has appeared to Simon!" Then they told what had happened on the road, and how he had been made known to them in the breaking of the bread.

Luke 24:14-55

I love the bible story of the Road to Emmaus for many different reasons. Here are three of them. First, it happens on a road. Many very important things seem to happen in the Christian scripture on the road to somewhere or another. Here, we are on the road to Emmaus, but there was a man on the road to Jericho who fell among thieves, the first line of the parable of the Good Samaritan. Saul of Tarsus, who persecuted Christians, became one. Where? On the Road to Damascus. Jesus, himself, was constantly on the move, traveling from one place to another. He said, "I am the Way," and early Christians were called people of the "Way." The way where, one might ask. The way to God or into the Kingdom of God, Christ might respond. We are all on a road, a spiritual road, just like Paul and the Good Samaritan. We may be at different places along the way, and we might enjoy different vistas, but we are all traveling a spiritual road.

Secondly, I like the story because it is about people we have never heard of before. Rather than being a story of Peter or Paul or James or John, major characters in the Christian narrative, it is a story about Cleopas and his unknown friend. This is Cleopas' only mention in the Christian scripture and to this day we don't know who his friend was. No doubt, they were early followers of Christ, but they weren't one of the twelve. They were common, ordinary, rank and file members of the group, not leaders, nobody special. The story tells us you don't have to be major player in the Gospel story to see the risen Christ. Christ can appear to plain, ordinary, rank and file folks, folks like you and me. This brings me to the third reason I like the story. I like it because Cleopas and his friend don't recognize Jesus.

Why didn't they? They knew him. They had seen him. They traveled with him. They knew of the women of their group who had seen the empty tomb. Why didn't they recognize Jesus? Maybe it was because Jesus did not look like what they expected the risen Christ to look like. He looked like a stranger. Maybe we must be alert to the people we meet along the way on our spiritual journey. The risen Christ may come to us in the form of a stranger, as someone different from us. He might not look like the great paintings of the Renaissance depicting the resurrected Christ. He might look more like the people in the pew next to us. He may be black or white. He may be rich or poor. He may be male or female. She may be an Episcopalian or a Southern Baptist. The next time our hearts are burning, let us consider for a moment that we just might be in the presence of the spirit of the risen Christ.

When we do, let us, like Cleopas and his friend, invite him to stay with us, offer him bread, let him break it and serve it to us so we too might recognize him in the breaking of the bread. For you see, he is risen. He walks the road with us. May we always be alert to his presence.

MR. ROGERS

J esus said, "I am the living bread that came down from heaven. Whoever eats of this bread will live forever; and the bread that I will give for the life of the world is my flesh."

The Jews then disputed among themselves, saying, "How can this man give us his flesh to eat?" So, Jesus said to them, "Very truly, I tell you, unless you eat the flesh of the Son of Man and drink his blood, you have no life in you. Those who eat my flesh and drink my blood have eternal life, and I will raise them up on the last day; for my flesh is true food and my blood is true drink. Those who eat my flesh and drink my blood abide in me, and I in them. Just as the living Father sent me, and I live because of the Father, so whoever eats me will live because of me. This is the bread that came down from heaven, not like that which your ancestors ate, and they died. But the one who eats this bread will live forever."

John 6:51-58

W hen I was 12 years old, I walked down this aisle, I climbed these chancel steps, I knelt at that alter rail where Bishop Vander Horst put his hands on my head and I was confirmed. Before Bishop Vander Horst did that, he required that I learn my catechism, and I did. But now 58 years later,

I have forgotten most of it.

The only thing I remember from my catechism is the definition of a sacrament. A sacrament is an outward and visible sign of an inward and spiritual grace. Confirmation, itself, is a sacrament, so when Bishop Vander Horst put his hands on my head, it was an outward and visible sign of an inward and spiritual grace.

As I read the lesson for today, I thought if you take the Bible literally, this passage is pretty gruesome. After all eating flesh and drinking blood is ghastly sounding when taken literally. But perhaps the words in our lesson today are sacramental. Maybe the words, themselves, are outward and visible signs or symbols of an inward and spiritual grace. Perhaps we should not give the words their literal meaning but their spiritual meaning.

For the last month you and I have been reading stories in John's gospel about being fed. It begins with the feeding of the 5000 and then goes on to stories about Jesus being the bread of life come down from heaven, saying we must eat his flesh and drink his blood to have an eternal life, a godly life, an infinitely deep life, a timeless life. Indeed, incorporating the body of Christ into our own body in the form of bread, and mixing the blood of Christ with our own blood in the form of wine, is an outward and visible sign of an inward and spiritual grace. It is a sign of the indwelling spirit of God and the spark of the divine we all share. When we eat the bread and drink the wine, we symbolically incorporate Christ into our own flesh and blood, and we become more Christ-like. We acknowledge the Christ within us. We have an eternal life. That is why communion is an outward and visible sign of an inward and spiritual grace.

Dan Matthews was the Assistant Rector here when I was confirmed. He told me that every individual has a basic need to love and to be loved. My favorite bible verse is from First John. "God is love and those that abide in love abide in God and god abides in them." Personally, I believe that love is not just a gift from God, it is God moving within us. It is the Christ within us. It is why we have that basic need to love and be loved. It is the inward and spiritual grace. And any ritual which points to God's indwelling presence in the form of love is sacramental. It is an outward and visible sign of an inward and spiritual grace and that grace is love.

Last week my wife and I went to see "Won't You Be my Neighbor" about Fred Rogers. In that movie, Mr. Rogers says, "The greatest thing that we can do is to help somebody know that they're loved and capable of loving." He says, "From the time you were very little, you've had people who have smiled you into smiling, people who have talked you into talking, sung you into singing, loved you into loving. So, on this day, let's take some time to think of those people. Some of them may be right here, some may be far away. Some may even be in heaven. No matter where they are, deep down you know they've always wanted what was best for you. They've always cared about you beyond measure and have encouraged you to be true to the best within you." Then Rogers states: "Let's just take a minute of silence to think about those people now."

And so, I, like Mr. Rogers, ask that in the silence that follows this reflection, let us perform Mr. Rogers' ritual, let us think of those people who have smiled us into smiling, talked us into talking, sung us into singing, and loved us into loving, because those people were living sacraments. They were an outward and visible sign of an inward and spiritual grace. May we also become living sacraments. As they were, let us be outward and visible signs of an inward and spiritual grace. In silence, we remember them.

SABBATH HEALING

One Sabbath Jesus and his disciples were going through the grainfields; and as they made their way his disciples began to pluck heads of grain. The Pharisees said to him, "Look, why are they doing what is not lawful on the Sabbath?" And he said to them, "Have you never read what David did when he and his companions were hungry and in need of food? He entered the house of God, when Abiathar was high priest, and ate the bread of the Presence, which it is not lawful for any but the priests to eat, and he gave some to his companions." Then he said to them, "The Sabbath was made for humankind, and not humankind for the Sabbath; so, the Son of Man is lord even of the Sabbath."

Again, he entered the synagogue, and a man was there who had a withered hand. They watched him to see whether he would cure him on the Sabbath, so that they might accuse him. And he said to the man who had the withered hand, "Come forward." Then he said to them, "Is it lawful to do good or to do harm on the Sabbath, to save life or to kill?" But they were silent. He looked around at them with anger; he was grieved at their hardness of heart and said to the man, "Stretch out your hand." He stretched it out, and his hand was restored. The Pharisees went out and immediately conspired with the Herodians against him, how to destroy him.

Mark 2:23-3:6

M ost of you know that I am a lawyer. That means by my nature, I am a rule follower. I help people know the rules and how to follow them, but sometimes people lose sight of the reason for the rule. They concentrate on the rule without any understanding why or how it came to be. They make the rule more important than the reasoning behind it. When that happens, rules become empty meaningless requirements. They become tyrannical. They become a form of idolatry. We begin to worship the letter of the law and ignore the spirit of the law. Under those circumstances, following the rule becomes a form of slavery.

Walter Brueggeman in his book, *Sabbath as Resistance*, taught me the reason for the Fourth Commandment. Remember the Sabbath and keep it holy. Okay, but why? The reason for Sabbath observance, according to Brueggeman, is to insure that there would be no slaves in the Promised Land. The children of Israel had been delivered from slavery. They had been led out of the land of Egypt. In Egypt, there was no day of rest for slaves, but in the Promised Land, there were no slaves. You can work 6 days, but on the seventh day, you shall not work. Why? Because we are slaves no longer.

How ironic that a commandment that was designed to free us, when blindly followed enslaves us. It becomes a "Thou shalt not" and stops being a "Thou may." It restricts us even though it was designed to free us. This is how evil works. Wolves in sheep's clothing use laws designed to protect us to enslave us.

Jesus knew the reason for the law. That is why he asks "Is it lawful to do good or to do harm on the Sabbath, to save life or to kill?" This is why he healed the man with the withered hand. The healing of this man freed him. It led him out of slavery. It was not something disallowed by the Sabbath like the Pharisees thought.

On the contrary, healing is required by the Sabbath.

One of my heroes is Henry David Thoreau. He wrote a famous essay called *Civil Disobedience*. That essay was read by Ghandi who later influenced Martin Luther King, Jr. He teaches us that some rules should be broken. Some laws lose sight of their purpose. Thoreau refused to pay his poll tax, and he was jailed for it. His good friend, Ralph Waldo Emerson visited him in jail and said to Thoreau, "Henry, what are you doing in there?" to which Thoreau replied, "Waldo, what are you doing out there?" Thoreau knew that some rules when they defeat their own purpose are not worthy of our obedience. He knew the poll tax designed to fund voting was denying people of the right to vote. Such a rule feeds upon itself until there is no real Sabbath and no real polling place and no real vote.

Our history is filled with thoughtful rule breakers. America cannot be an independent country. Why is that? Because it's the rule. You can't throw that tea in the harbor. Why not? It's the rule. You can't be ordained a priest. You're a woman! Why? That's the rule. Don't you know the rules!? And gay people can't be priests either. It's the rule.

Now, don't get me wrong. I believe in rules. I am a rule follower, but let us not allow rules designed to free us enslave us. My friends, we live in a country, the land of the free and the home of the brave, where children are being separated from their parents at our border because of the rules. We have children being murdered in their classrooms, and we can do nothing about it because of the rules? But, my friends, we are not slaves. We have been delivered from Egypt. There are no slaves in the Promised Land! Jesus teaches us that the Sabbath was made for humankind, and not humankind for the Sabbath. So too our laws were made for humankind and not humankind for the law. Remember the Sabbath. It is holy. It frees us. Let us keep it holy and liberating.

WOUNDS

Jesus himself stood among the disciples and said to them, "Peace be with you." They were startled and terrified, and thought that they were seeing a ghost. He said to them, "Why are you frightened, and why do doubts arise in your hearts? Look at my hands and my feet; see that it is I myself. Touch me and see; for a ghost does not have flesh and bones as you see that I have." And when he had said this, he showed them his hands and his feet. While in their joy they were disbelieving and still wondering, he said to them, "Have you anything here to eat?" They gave him a piece of broiled fish, and he took it and ate in their presence.

Then he said to them, "These are my words that I spoke to you while I was still with you—that everything written about me in the law of Moses, the prophets, and the psalms must be fulfilled." Then he opened their minds to understand the scriptures, and he said to them, "Thus it is written, that the Messiah is to suffer and to rise from the dead on the third day, and that repentance and forgiveness of sins is to be proclaimed in his name to all nations, beginning from Jerusalem. You are witnesses of these things.

Luke 24:36-38

Richard Rohr comments, in one of his podcasts, that if he had written the gospels, he would resurrect Jesus in a pristine condition. The holes in his hands and feet and the wound in his side would be miraculously healed in the Gospel according to Richard. Certainly, if Jesus could overcome death, heal lepers, bring sight to blind, and hearing to the deaf, a few nail holes and a stab wound would have been child's play by comparison. But it wouldn't have made as good a story, says Rohr. No, the resurrected Jesus comes to us in a wounded state.

Indeed, his wounds are his calling card. Are you a ghost or is this really you? We're not sure, the disciples say. We're going to need to see some sort of identification, and what does Jesus show them as identification? He shows them his wounds. Look at my hands and feet and see that it is I, myself. His wounds convince the disciples that that this is, indeed, Jesus. Jesus' identity is seen in his wounds. Even at the height of his glory, he retains his wounds. My friends, you and I follow a wounded messiah.

I have learned from theoretical physicists that prior to the Big Bang, all matter, the entire universe was contained in an infinitesimally small particle called the singularity. This singularity exploded at the moment of creation. I like to think that singularity is God. I like to think God exploded into the void at creation. God sacrificed his singularity for our sake. My friends, we worship a sacrificed, broken God. We follow a wounded messiah, and we worship a sacrificed God, a broken God, a God broken in the act of our own creation. And we are the remnants, the pieces of that broken God.

Paul writes, "We preach Christ crucified! We preach strength can come from weakness. We preach power can come from vulnerability because a wounded Christ reflects our own wounds. A broken God can be seen in our brokenness. As Rumi put it, our wounds are the places where the light enters into us. The Word, the Logos, the image of God has, quite literally, become flesh and dwells among us.

I think I can say without fear of contradiction that we all, lay and clergy alike, have experienced a dark night of the soul. We have all experienced a death of spirit, and we have been wounded. But with the help of God and the love of family and friends, we emerge on the other side of our suffering stronger and closer to God than ever before. We are resurrected in a sense. But our wounds are still with us. They don't ever go away. Despite resurrection, they remain to remind us of our shared suffering, our kinship with Christ as children of God. Let us honor our wounds, our little sacrifices. They strengthen us. They identify us. We learn from them. They make us who we are. They are our calling card. May the followers of a wounded messiah and the worshippers of a broken God, see Christ's wounds as a mirror image of our own. Let us, like Christ, be resurrected with our wounds. May we, like God, find creation in our brokenness.

THE CALL OF CHRIST

After John was arrested, Jesus came to Galilee, proclaiming the good news of God, and saying, "The time is fulfilled, and the kingdom of God has come near; repent, and believe in the good news."

As Jesus passed along the Sea of Galilee, he saw Simon and his brother Andrew casting a net into the sea—for they were fishermen. And Jesus said to them, "Follow me and I will make you fish for people." And immediately they left their nets and followed him. As he went a little farther, he saw James son of Zebedee and his brother John, who were in their boat mending the nets. Immediately he called them; and they left their father Zebedee in the boat with the hired men, and followed him.

Mark 1:14-20

One snowy day, I stayed home from work. My wife was working on one of her projects and was totally unavailable to entertain me. I soon became bored cooped up in the house with nothing to do. So, I turned on the TV and began cruising through the endless list of programming when I stumbled upon one of my favorite movies, "The Verdict" with Paul Newman. I hate lawyer movies. Being a lawyer, I'm too quick to see the fallacies in them. But "The Verdict" is different. It is a fairly accurate depiction of a trial and trial preparation.

The movie was almost over. It was at the part where attorney Frank Galvin, gives his summation to the jury. It's the best summation I have ever heard. He doesn't talk about the facts of the case, but only speaks of faith and justice.

He rises and softly says: "Well...You know, so much of the time we're just lost. We say, 'Please, God, tell us what is right. Tell us what is true.'

"I mean there is no justice. The rich win; the poor are powerless. We become tired of hearing people lie. And after a time, we become dead, a little dead. We think of ourselves as victims -- and we become victims. We become weak; we doubt ourselves; we doubt our beliefs; we doubt our institutions; and we doubt the law. But today you are the law. You are the law, not some book, not the lawyers, not a marble statue, or the trappings of the court. See, those are just symbols of our desire to be just. They are, in fact, a prayer, a fervent and a frightened prayer.

"In my religion, they say, 'Act as if you had faith; faith will be given to you.' If we are to have faith in justice, we need only to believe in ourselves and act with justice. See, I believe there is justice in our hearts."

And that's it. That's his summation.

I can hear Christ calling me in Galvin's summation. I, too, sometimes feel there is no justice. The rich win, the poor are powerless. I too become tired of hearing people lie, but then Christ calls me, and when I say Christ, I am using that term as Richard Rohr uses it, the cosmic, universal Christ, the Christ of faith, the everlasting presence of God in all things.

That Christ was in Jesus. It's in me. It's in each of you. It's in all of creation, and it calls us from deep within ourselves, from the very essence of our being because Christ is the highest and best within us. That Christ calls to me every time I read the Memphis Commercial Appeal or the New York Times or listen to CNN. That Christ calls us just as Christ called Simon and his brother, Andrew, and James and John. Christ calls us as if we were sitting in our fishing boat next to our father Zebedee mending our nets by the Sea of Galilee. Christ calls us. Christ says to us, "Get out of that pew. Walk out of that church and do something to advance the coming of the kingdom. Christ says, "The time is fulfilled, the kingdom of God is near; repent, and believe this good news." "Follow me," he says. "Become fishers of people," because, my friends, people are drowning in the Sea of Galilee in front of our very eyes.

"In my religion, they say, 'Act as if you had faith; faith will be given to you.' If we are to have faith in justice, we need only to believe in ourselves and act with justice. See, I believe there is justice in our hearts." There is Christ in our hearts. The everlasting presence of the spirit of God is in our hearts, and it is calling to us in the silence.

THE CANAANITE WOMAN

J esus left that place and went away to the district of Tyre and Sidon. Just then a Canaanite woman from that region came out and started shouting, "Have mercy on me, Lord, Son of David; my daughter is tormented by a demon." But he did not answer her at all. And his disciples came and urged him, saying, "Send her away, for she keeps shouting after us." He answered, "I was sent only to the lost sheep of the house of Israel." But she came and knelt before him, saying, "Lord, help me." He answered, "It is not fair to take the children's food and throw it to the dogs." She said, "Yes, Lord, yet even the dogs eat the crumbs that fall from their masters' table." Then Jesus answered her, "Woman, great is your faith! Let it be done for you as you wish." And her daughter was healed instantly.

Matthew 15: 21-28

R ichard Rohr writes a lot about the "Cosmic Christ." This is a term coined by Matthew Fox, a Dominican friar who was expelled by the Catholic Church and became an Episcopal priest. He originated Creation Theology which views all of creation as a physical manifestation of God and, therefore, holy. The human family being part of creation is part of that holy manifestation of God. We have been created in the image and likeness of God. As Emerson put it, "We have within us the wise silence, the soul of the whole, the universal beauty, to which every part and particle is equally related, the eternal one." Marcus Borg called it Panentheism, not Pantheism which is the worship of nature, but Panentheism which is the belief that God is in all nature and all creation. Rohr defines the Cosmic Christ as the universal and everlasting presence of God in all things. It was in Jesus, and it is within each of us. We can see it, if we choose, in everything we behold.

Today's lesson is troubling. Jesus behaved pretty badly toward the Canaanite woman. He refuses to help her saying it is not fair to take the children's food and throw it to Canaanite dogs. His statement is a reflection of the 2000 years of animosity between Israelites and Canaanites. When Joshua fought the battle of Jericho it was the Canaanites he was fighting. Canaanites did not worship Yahweh, the God of Israel, but Baal, a god equated with the devil. They did not keep the Mosaic Laws. It is no wonder that friction existed between Jews and Canaanites.

And yet, this is actually what makes the passage so topical. Not much has changed in 2000 years. We still suffer from the same tribalism that separated the Jews and the Canaanites. One need look no further than Charlottesville, Virginia and our present political climate to realize that tribalism is alive and well in America. We have just changed the names of the tribes. Today, we call them Democrats or Republicans, straight or gay, Protestant or Catholic, Black or White. These are the tribes of the 21st century.

But Jesus and the Canaanite woman overcame tribalism. Matthew's story is a case of joint and mutual salvation. It is a shared healing. The Christ in the Canaanite woman reaches out and recognizes the Christ in Jesus. "Have mercy on me, lord, son of David," and the Christ in Jesus, in turn, recognizes the Christ in her. "Your faith is great. Let it be as you wish."

But what is faith? I would say it is the recognition of the holy in our lives coupled with our persistence in connecting with it. The Canaanite woman was nothing if she wasn't persistent. "Send her away, she keeps shouting at us," say the disciples. This reminds me of the story of the hemophiliac woman. She, like the Canaanite woman, was persistent when she reached out and touched the fringe of Jesus' garment. "Your faith has healed you," Jesus tells her. Not, I have healed you, but your faith has healed you. She recognized the holy, made contact and was healed.

The blind beggar Bartimaeus waited for days for Jesus to come near. Bartimaeus like the Canaanite woman was persistent. Again, Jesus said, "Your faith has healed you." if Bartimaeus' faith healed him and if the hemophiliac woman's faith healed her, maybe our faith can heal us. If we recognize the holy all around us and are persistent in making contact with it, maybe we, too, can be healed.

If we are Christians, if we follow Jesus, let us follow him to the region of Tyre and Sidon. Let us encounter a Canaanite woman there, someone who is different from us, someone who speaks another language, someone whose religion is different from ours and may we see the Christ in her, and may she see the Christ in us so that we can both be healed of this disease, this sin of tribalism.

NOT PEACE BUT
A SWORD

J esus said to the twelve disciples, "A disciple is not above the teacher, nor a slave above the master; it is enough for the disciple to be like the teacher, and the slave like the master. If they have called the master of the house Beelzebub, how much more will they malign those of his household!

"So have no fear of them; for nothing is covered up that will not be uncovered, and nothing secret that will not become known. What I say to you in the dark, tell in the light; and what you hear whispered, proclaim from the housetops. Do not fear those who kill the body but cannot kill the soul; rather fear him who can destroy both soul and body in hell. Are not two sparrows sold for a penny? Yet not one of them will fall to the ground apart from your Father. And even the hairs of your head are all counted. So do not be afraid; you are of more value than many sparrows.

"Everyone therefore who acknowledges me before others, I also will acknowledge before my Father in heaven; but whoever denies me before others, I also will deny before my Father in heaven.

"Do not think that I have come to bring peace to the earth; I have not come to bring peace, but a sword.

For I have come to set a man against his father, and a daughter against her mother, and a daughter-in-law against her mother-in-law; and one's foes will be members of one's own household.

Whoever loves father or mother more than me is not worthy of me; and whoever loves son or daughter more than me is not worthy of me; and whoever does not take up the cross and follow me is not worthy of me. Those who find their life will lose it, and those who lose their life for my sake will find it."

Matthew 10:24-39

Sometimes when I read a verse of scripture there is a word or a phrase that just leaps off the page at me. Today's gospel was like that. "I have not come to bring peace, but a sword." "Really", I thought? You have not come to bring peace but a sword? This from the same Jesus who told his disciples in the shuttered room three times, "Peace be with you?" This from the same Jesus who said in John's Gospel, "Peace I leave with you, my peace I give to you?" In just a few moments you and I will greet each other with the ancient Christian greeting, "May the peace of the Lord be with you" and the ancient Christian response, "and also with you," and now we read, "I come not to bring peace but a sword." Are these the words of Isaiah's Prince of Peace? I daresay that you will never see those words etched inside a Christmas card any time soon.

Yes, those words leapt off the page at me. Why? Because this is not the meek, mild, lamb-carrying Jesus that I learned about in my childhood.

Then, I remembered the words of a minister friend of mine. She told the story of being at a cocktail party when a new acquaintance asked her, "What do you do for a living."

"I am a minister," she replied," He said, "Your faith must be a source of great comfort to you" and she said, "No, actually, it's not. Actually, it is a source of great discomfort to me. It's like I am constantly being poked with a sharp stick!" The Archbishop of Canterbury once said, "The purpose of all religion is to comfort the afflicted and to afflict the comfortable." Maybe this sword that Christ brings, is pointed toward us. Maybe it is the self-same sharp stick, my minister friend speaks of. Maybe it is there, to afflict us in our comfort.

But where is this peace that Christ promises us? How does that actually work? Maybe it comes to us through our afflictions. I have seen people cross deep, stormy seas of trouble only to emerge on the other side with their faith deepened. An alcoholic can only achieve sobriety after he hits bottom, after he has fallen so low that he has no other choice but to change, and change, my friends, is traumatic. It is not easy. Spiritual transformation is not for sissies. The road to heaven often leads through hell. There can be no Easter without a Good Friday, BUT It is from the fire of the forge that the tempered steel of faith emerges.

The Episcopal denomination has not been without controversy. The ordination of women and gay priests and same sex marriage have all been sources of friction.   They have, quite literally, set a man against his father, and a daughter against her mother, and a daughter-in-law against her mother-in-law; and one's foes were members of one's own household. But we have emerged from each controversy with our faith crystallized, with a new understanding of the plight of others and a renewed love of neighbor.

I know that some of you are in deep sorrow. You may suffer with illness. You may be dealing with addiction. You may be experiencing great disappointment. You may be mourning the death of a loved one, but during these times of darkness the light and love of God sits with us in our afflictions. God weeps with us. For you see, the Good News of Jesus Christ is true. The Kingdom of God IS near. It's as near as the person in the pew next to you. It's as near as your own heartbeat, but getting there is not easy. Jesus never said it would be. The way into the kingdom is inundated with sharp sticks. And so, I say to you, in spite of your trials, indeed, because of them, work always to advance the coming of the kingdom. Look for God's grace in your life, be open to the in-dwelling Holy Spirit even in your afflictions, and the peace of the Lord just may finally come to you.

CHOICES

Now there was a Pharisee named Nicodemus, a leader of the Jews. He came to Jesus by night and said to him, "Rabbi, we know that you are a teacher who has come from God; for no one can do these signs that you do apart from the presence of God." Jesus answered him, "Very truly, I tell you, no one can see the kingdom of God without being born from above." Nicodemus said to him, "How can anyone be born after having grown old? Can one enter a second time into the mother's womb and be born?" Jesus answered, "Very truly, I tell you, no one can enter the kingdom of God without being born of water and Spirit. What is born of the flesh is flesh, and what is born of the Spirit is spirit. Do not be astonished that I said to you, 'You must be born from above.' The wind blows where it chooses, and you hear the sound of it, but you do not know where it comes from or where it goes. So it is with everyone who is born of the Spirit." Nicodemus said to him, "How can these things be?" Jesus answered him, "Are you a teacher of Israel, and yet you do not understand these things?

"Very truly, I tell you, we speak of what we know and testify to what we have seen; yet you do not receive our testimony. If I have told you about earthly things and you do not believe, how can you believe if I tell you about heavenly things? No one has ascended into heaven except the one who descended from heaven, the Son of Man. And just as Moses lifted up the serpent in the wilderness, so must the Son of Man be lifted up, that whoever believes in him may have eternal life.

"For God so loved the world that he gave his only Son, so that everyone who believes in him may not perish but may have eternal life.

"Indeed, God did not send the Son into the world to condemn the world, but in order that the world might be saved through him."

John 3:1-17

Two roads diverged in a yellow wood,
And sorry I could not travel both
And be one traveler, long I stood
And looked down one as far as I could
To where it bent in the undergrowth;

Then took the other, as just as fair,
And having perhaps the better claim,
Because it was grassy and wanted wear;
Though as for that the passing there
Had worn them really about the same,

And both that morning equally lay
In leaves no step had trodden black.
Oh, I kept the first for another day!
Yet knowing how way leads on to way,
I doubted if I should ever come back.

I shall be telling this with a sigh
Somewhere ages and ages hence:
Two roads diverged in a wood, and I—
I took the one less traveled by,
And that has made all the difference.

Robert Frost's The Road Not Taken. I had always interpreted this poem to mean that choices are important. But then I read that Frost had a friend who agonized over every choice and that Frost's poem was a tongue in cheek critique of his friend who was too frozen by fear to make choices. It was Frost's way of saying make your choice and move on because choices aren't that important. So, which is it? Choices are important? Choices aren't important? Isn't it exquisitely delicious that we have a choice of interpretations regarding a poem about choices?

I told my wife about the second but opposite interpretation of Frost's poem and she said, "I don't like that interpretation. I like the first one. Choices are important." I agree with her.

We make choices all the time, don't we? Where do we go to school? Who will be our friends? Whom shall we marry? What job will we take? Whom should we vote for? Yes, choices are important.

Nicodemus had to make choices, didn't he? He only appears in John's Gospel, not just once, but three times. First here, then later when he stood up for Jesus before the Sanhedrin and lastly when he prepared Jesus' body for burial.

Nicodemus was a Pharisee, and we all know what Jesus thought of Pharisees. He was a member of the Sanhedrin, the council that tried and convicted Jesus. Maybe that's why he visits Jesus by night, fearful of being seen. But later in John's Gospel everyone heard him speak up for Jesus before the Sanhedrin and everyone saw him receive Jesus' body. Nicodemus made choices, unpopular choices. He made choices that exposed him to criticism at the very same time Peter, the rock upon which the Church would be built, was denying Jesus three times. Nicodemus was, quite literally, transformed from a Pharisee into a disciple of Christ.

Maybe there's still hope for Pharisees like me, Pharisees like us who insist on strict observance of the rules, who hesitate to rock the boat, to buck the established system, who do things because that is the way they've always been done.

Yes, we make choices. How will we respond to refugees? How will we act toward Muslims? How will we treat members of the LGBT community? Yes, we make choices not only as individuals but also as a church. Sometimes the choosing is not easy. Like Frost's friend, we may be frozen by fear. At first, the timid Nicodemus within us, might have to visit the courageous Christ within us by the dark of night, but it is my hope that we make these choices, not as Pharisees but as transformed disciples of Christ who have been born from above because no one can **see**, much less enter, the Kingdom of God **without** being born from above.

Two roads diverged in a wood, and I, *and we—*
We took the one less traveled by,
And that has made all the difference.

Amen.

THE LAMB OF GOD

John saw Jesus coming toward him and declared, "Here is the Lamb of God who takes away the sin of the world! This is he of whom I said, 'After me comes a man who ranks ahead of me because he was before me.' I myself did not know him; but I came baptizing with water for this reason, that he might be revealed to Israel." And John testified, "I saw the Spirit descending from heaven like a dove, and it remained on him. I myself did not know him, but the one who sent me to baptize with water said to me, 'He on whom you see the Spirit descend and remain is the one who baptizes with the Holy Spirit.' And I myself have seen and have testified that this is the Son of God."

The next day John again was standing with two of his disciples, and as he watched Jesus walk by, he exclaimed, "Look, here is the Lamb of God!" The two disciples heard him say this, and they followed Jesus. When Jesus turned and saw them following, he said to them, "What are you looking for?" They said to him, "Rabbi" (which translated means Teacher), "where are you staying?" He said to them, "Come and see." They came and saw where he was staying, and they remained with him that day. It was about four o'clock in the afternoon. One of the two who heard John speak and followed him was Andrew, Simon Peter's brother. He first found his brother Simon and said to him, "We have found the Messiah" (which is translated Anointed). He brought Simon to Jesus, who looked at him and said, "You are Simon son of John. You are to be called Cephas" (which is translated Peter).

John 1:29-42

W hat exactly is the sin of the world and how is it taken away by this lamb of God? Sin is such a loaded word. There are two definitions of sin that I like. The first one is that sin is disobedience to God's will. The second is that sin is anything that alienates us or separates us from God. Sin is disobedience, alienation and separation from God.

Many good Christians read this gospel lesson as support for the doctrine of substitutionary atonement, that God sent Jesus to die on the cross to atone for our sins. It was we who deserved death, but it was Jesus who died on the cross for our sins. Anselm of Canterbury developed this interpretation around 1034, but during the first thousand years of Christianity the doctrine of substitutionary atonement was unknown. Most early Christians would understand the Jesus story in terms of transformation through the incarnation of the Holy Spirit. Irenaeus, the first bishop of Lyon, said around the year 200, 800 years before Anselm, "God became like us so that we could become like Him." He said, "The Glory of God is a human being fully alive." To Irenaeus, the Spirit became carnate in Jesus and we too, through Christ, have received the Holy Spirit. If we acknowledge it and nurture it, we can grow more and more into the image and likeness of God. In this way, the Spirit transforms us, just as it transformed Jesus. It can take away the sin of the world. If disobedience to God's will is sin, Jesus takes it away by showing us what obedience looks like, even obedience unto death. If the sin of the world is alienation and separation from God, Jesus takes it away by dwelling among us, by the gift of the Holy Spirit, by bringing God down from the mountaintop of the Hebrew scripture and placing him where he belongs, squarely in the human heart.

Jesus is the lamb of God writ large and we, if we follow Christ, if we have been transformed by the incarnation of the holy Spirit, become lambs of god writ small. We, too, must recognize the Holy Spirit within us, the Christ within us, and be willing to sacrifice our pride and our egos to that indwelling spirit so that we can be obedient, as Christ was obedient, to God's will for us.

I do not believe that it is by chance that the story of the lamb of God is coupled with the call of Andrew and Peter. Jesus asks Andrew, "What are you looking for?" The question travels across two thousand years and thousands of miles from Christ's lips to our ears. What, indeed, ARE we looking for? "Where are you staying?" Indeed, where is Christ staying? The verb staying is the same verb used earlier when John observes the Spirit remaining on Jesus. A better translation is abiding or enduring. We should ask ourselves, where is Christ abiding, where is Christ enduring. Jesus' answer to Andrew's question invites us into communion with him. He says, "Come and See." The many stories of Jesus healing the blind so that they can see makes these words so meaningful. Indeed, come and see now that we have been given light.

What I think Andrew was looking for is the same thing we are looking for in this season of Epiphany, communion, communion with God, a Holy Communion, if you will allow the use of that term. If the sin of the world is alienation from God, the salvation of the world is communion with God. So let us be transformed by the incarnation of the Holy Spirit. Let us enter into a holy communion. May we, like Andrew, accept Jesus' invitation to come and see.

BE WORTHY OF
YOUR REPENTENCE

In those days John the Baptist appeared in the wilderness of Judea, proclaiming, "Repent, for the kingdom of heaven has come near." This is the one of whom the prophet Isaiah spoke when he said,

> "The voice of one crying out in the wilderness:
> 'Prepare the way of the Lord,
>   make his paths straight.'"

Now John wore clothing of camel's hair with a leather belt around his waist, and his food was locusts and wild honey. Then the people of Jerusalem and all Judea were going out to him, and all the region along the Jordan, and they were baptized by him in the river Jordan, confessing their sins.

But when he saw many Pharisees and Sadducees coming for baptism, he said to them, "You brood of vipers! Who warned you to flee from the wrath to come? Bear fruit worthy of repentance. Do not presume to say to yourselves, 'We have Abraham as our ancestor'; for I tell you, God is able from these stones to raise up children to Abraham. Even now the ax is lying at the root of the trees; every tree therefore that does not bear good fruit is cut down and thrown into the fire.

"I baptize you with water for repentance, but one who is more powerful than I is coming after me; I am not worthy to carry his sandals. He will baptize you with the Holy Spirit and fire. His winnowing fork is in his hand, and he will clear his threshing floor and will gather his wheat into the granary; but the chaff he will burn with unquenchable fire."

Matthew 3:1-12

When I was a teenager, I would ask my father if I could borrow his car to take my date to the movies on Friday or Saturday night. As he handed me the keys, he would always say the same thing. He said it every time. It became so habitual that I would say it right along with him knowing it was coming. He and I would say in unison, "Son, remember you're a Huguenot."

Some of you may know that the Huguenots were Protestants living in Catholic France during the Protestant Reformation. It was not good to be a Huguenot in those days, especially on the day of August 24, 1572, the feast day of Saint Bartholomew. That was the day thousands of Huguenots were murdered by their Catholic countrymen during France's wars of religion. They say the streets of Paris ran red with blood that day, Huguenot blood. It was called the Saint Bartholomew's Day Massacre.

Many Huguenots fled to the new world, and most of them settled in South Carolina where my father, one of their descendants, was born. My father was very proud of his Huguenot ancestry as well he should be. Indeed, there are many famous Huguenots in America. Davy Crockett, Judy Garland, Henry Wadsworth Longfellow, Tyrone Power, Charlize Theron, Henry David Thoreau, John Greenleaf Whittier, Warren Buffet, E. I. Du Pont, Howard Hughes, Francis Marion, John D. Rockefeller, Tom Brokaw, George S. Patton,

Paul Revere, Winston Churchill, Alexander Hamilton, Sarah Palin, and Franklin D. Roosevelt are all descended from Huguenots. My father would be proud to be associated with some if not all of these.

But you see when my father told me to remember that I was a Huguenot, he was not asking me to recollect some martyred French men. No, he was asking me to be faithful to the highest and best within me because to my father being a Huguenot represented the highest and the best within himself. In religious terms, we Christians might call it being faithful to the Christ within us because Christ is the highest and best within us. He was extolling me not just to remember that I was a Huguenot. He was challenging me to *be* a Huguenot by emulating my hero ancestors. It was his way of saying bring that car back to me in the same shape I gave it to you. Don't go, as he liked to say, joy-riding. You see, he was worried about what I might do with his car. He was saying be a good steward of my brand new, 1965, Buick Lesabre!

You see, in the last analysis, it matters not what group we identify with. What matters is what we do, how we act, how we love, regardless of our group identification. What our ancestors *did* is the very reason we honor them. Christ, himself, said, "By their deeds you shall know them." If John the Baptizer were here today, he might say to me do not presume to say to yourself, "I have a Huguenot as my ancestor" for I tell you God is able from these stones to raise up sons of Huguenots. God can raise up from these stones sons and daughters of Episcopalians or Unitarians or Democrats or Republicans or Americans for that matter.

Certainly, we can be proud to share the faith of Matthew, Mark, Luke, John, Paul and Christ, himself, and, yes, we should indeed emulate them. But do not think that our privileged place in any group or any race or any church alone redeems us. It doesn't. What matters is what we do; how we love. What matters is that we must be faithful to the highest and best within us, to the Christ within us. In this season of Advent, we are asked to be looking for the coming of the Christ within us, the highest and best within us. John says repent or, perhaps a better translation, be transformed by this baptism you have received of the Holy Spirit and bear fruit worthy of your repentance. Bear fruit worthy of your transformation. Bear fruit worthy of the advent of Christ within you, bear fruit worthy of your baptism with the Holy Spirit.

FIRE AND ICE

Jesus entered Jericho and was passing through it. A man was there named Zacchaeus; he was a chief tax collector and was rich. He was trying to see who Jesus was, but on account of the crowd he could not, because he was short in stature. So, he ran ahead and climbed a sycamore tree to see him, because he was going to pass that way. When Jesus came to the place, he looked up and said to him, "Zacchaeus, hurry and come down; for I must stay at your house today." So, he hurried down and was happy to welcome him. All who saw it began to grumble and said, "He has gone to be the guest of one who is a sinner." Zacchaeus stood there and said to the Lord, "Look, half of my possessions, Lord, I will give to the poor; and if I have defrauded anyone of anything, I will pay back four times as much." Then Jesus said to him, "Today salvation has come to this house, because he too is a son of Abraham. For the Son of Man came to seek out and to save the lost."

Luke 19:1-10

Some say the world will end in fire,
Some say in ice.
From what I've tasted of desire
I hold with those who favor fire.
But if it had to perish twice,
I think I know enough of hate
To say that for destruction ice
Is also great

And would suffice.

Y ou may recognize Robert Frost's short, power-packed poem, *Fire and Ice*. You and I have seen a lot of fire and ice in the past year, haven't we? The killing of unarmed Blacks. The murder of police officers, tawdry tales of sexual assault, a toxic campaign filled with vitriol. Every time you turn on the TV all you hear is fire and ice. Every time you pick up a newspaper, its fire and ice, fire and ice.

The Gospel this evening gives us some respite from fire and ice. The story of Zacchaeus who was trying to see Jesus, but could not because people blocked his line of sight. So, he ran ahead to a place where he knew Jesus would pass and climbed a tree so he could see Jesus. And not only could he see Jesus, but Jesus saw him and invited himself into Zacchaeus' home and through that encounter with the Christ, Zacchaeus was transformed.

Maybe this story is more complicated than a silly tale of a wee little tax collector in a tree. Maybe this story is really about you and me. Perhaps, we are all people of short stature, spiritually speaking. Perhaps there are people or things that obstruct our spiritual vision. Perhaps you and I need to be running ahead and climbing Sycamore trees so we can see the approaching Christ, and when we do, perhaps Christ will invite himself into our homes and we, like Zacchaeus, will be transformed.

And when I say the word, Christ, I am not just referring to the man, Jesus. I am talking about something much bigger than that. I am talking about what Richard Rohr calls the Cosmic Christ, the preexistent Christ that the gospeler John referred to when he wrote, "In the beginning was the Word, and the Word was with God, and the Word was God." I am talking about the Logos, the mind of God, the Peace of God, the Love of God. I am talking about Christ as Richard Rohr defines Christ. Christ to him is the everlasting presence of God in all things, the admixture of Spirit and matter for which Jesus gives us a very fragrant focal point. It is this Christ that approaches us, and it is this Christ that we most desperately need to see in ourselves and others.

In this toxic campaign season, the acerbic vitriol can change us both as individuals and as a nation, and not necessarily for the better. But it also gives us an opportunity, a wonderful opportunity to practice our faith by being able to see the approaching Christ even in those people who disagree with us, even in those people who support the other candidate, even in people of difference races, even people we grumble about, like the people grumbled about Zacchaeus.

You see the problem with Frost's poem, *Fire and Ice*, is that it points out the problem but it offers no solution for the fire and ice all around us. The antidote for the poison of fire and ice is the Logos, the Peace of God, the Love of God, the preexistent Christ, the Cosmic Christ, the Christ that dwells within us and within our enemies. That Christ quenches fire. That Christ thaws ice, if we would but only see.

So, let us exert ourselves. Let us practice our faith. Let us run ahead and climb that Sycamore tree so that we, too, can finally see the approaching Christ in ourselves and others and by that new vision may we be transformed.

SET YOUR FACES

When the days drew near for Jesus to be taken up, he set his face to go to Jerusalem. And he sent messengers ahead of him. On their way they entered a village of the Samaritans to make ready for him; but they did not receive him, because his face was set toward Jerusalem. When his disciples James and John saw it, they said, "Lord, do you want us to command fire to come down from heaven and consume them?" But he turned and rebuked them. Then they went on to another village.

As they were going along the road, someone said to him, "I will follow you wherever you go." And Jesus said to him, "Foxes have holes, and birds of the air have nests; but the Son of Man has nowhere to lay his head." To another he said, "Follow me." But he said, "Lord, first let me go and bury my father." But Jesus said to him, "Let the dead bury their own dead; but as for you, go and proclaim the kingdom of God." Another said, "I will follow you, Lord; but let me first say farewell to those at my home." Jesus said to him, "No one who puts a hand to the plow and looks back is fit for the kingdom of God."

Luke 9:51-62

He set his face for Jerusalem. What a powerful expression. It evokes a sense of determination and dedication. Jesus was going to Jerusalem no matter what. He was bound and determined to go there regardless of the consequences. And we all know, because we've read ahead, we all know what awaits Jesus in Jerusalem. We know how he confronts the Temple authorities, we all know how he drove out the money changers, how he was arrested, how he was tried by Pilate, how he was flogged, and how he was crucified. Why was Jesus so eager to go to Jerusalem to face torture and death? Perhaps, at times, he wasn't.

One of the most poignant prayers in all Christian Scripture is found at Luke 22:42-44, "Father, if You are willing, take this cup from Me. Yet not My will, but Yours be done." Then, the scripture continues, ". . . an angel from heaven appeared to Him and strengthened Him. And in His anguish, He prayed more earnestly, and His sweat became like drops of blood falling to the ground. . . ."

I have prayed that same prayer. Father, if you are willing, take this cup from me. It's too hard. I can't do it. And I imagine many of you have prayed that prayer, too. In just a few moments you and I will pray the Lord's Prayer together with its most daunting declaration: "Thy will be done". Easy to utter, but difficult to accept sometimes, God's will for us.

Being a Christian is not all sweetness and light. It has a sharp edge to it. Just ask Dietrich Bonhoeffer who was hanged by the Nazis for participating in a plot to assassinate Hitler. Just ask Oscar Romero, the priest, who was gunned down in his own church for preaching against the government. Just ask Martin Luther King, Jr. dead from an assassin's bullet. Just ask all the Christian martyrs down through the ages.

But despite the danger, we must imitate Christ. We must set our faces toward Jerusalem. And here I need to ask you a question: Just exactly, where is this Jerusalem, this Holy City, where God dwells in his Holy Temple. Perhaps Jerusalem is not a city in the Middle East. Perhaps, like Bethlehem, Jerusalem is a place in the human heart. The collect assigned for today says, "Grant . . . that we may be made a holy temple acceptable to you." Paul says our bodies are the temple of the Holy Spirit. This Jerusalem, this holy city where God dwells, is within us and it calls to us with that wee small voice within. That call often frightens us. Sometimes, it can challenge us beyond our ability to respond, but if we answer that call, it will transform us. It will transform us. If we set our faces against the modern-day demons of addiction, fear, and loneliness, if we set our faces toward loving perceived enemies, if we are faithful to God's will for us, we can cast out the money changers of our hearts, we can cleanse this Temple within us. You see, today's Gospel is a call story. Christ is calling us from this scripture. Follow me, says Jesus, and it's not going be easy, so set your faces, and follow me to the holy city within you. Amen,

BREATHING

When it was evening on that day, the first day of the week, and the doors of the house where the disciples had met were locked for fear of the Jews, Jesus came and stood among them and said, "Peace be with you." After he said this, he showed them his hands and his side. Then the disciples rejoiced when they saw the Lord. Jesus said to them again, "Peace be with you. As the Father has sent me, so I send you." When he had said this, he breathed on them and said to them, "Receive the Holy Spirit. If you forgive the sins of any, they are forgiven them; if you retain the sins of any, they are retained."

But Thomas (who was called the Twin), one of the twelve, was not with them when Jesus came. So, the other disciples told him, "We have seen the Lord." But he said to them, "Unless I see the mark of the nails in his hands, and put my finger in the mark of the nails and my hand in his side, I will not believe."

A week later his disciples were again in the house, and Thomas was with them. Although the doors were shut, Jesus came and stood among them and said, "Peace be with you." Then he said to Thomas, "Put your finger here and see my hands. Reach out your hand and put it in my side. Do not doubt but believe." Thomas answered him, "My Lord and my God!" Jesus said to him, "Have you believed because you have seen me? Blessed are those who have not seen and yet have come to believe."

Now Jesus did many other signs in the presence of his disciples, which are not written in this book. But these are written so that you may come to believe that Jesus is the Messiah, the Son of God, and that through believing you may have life in his name.

John 20:19-31

When I read this Gospel story I said, "This is inconsistent. This says that disciples received the Holy Spirit when Jesus breathed on them in the shuttered room, but the Book of Acts says the Holy Spirit came to the disciples on the day of Pentecost, fifty days later. That's inconsistent. Which is it? It's got to be one or the other, right?"

Well perhaps not. Perhaps, I've concluded, the Spirit can come to different people at different times in different ways. I think we can receive the Spirit, then lose it, then gain it again. I would say that Jesus did not so much give us the Holy Spirit as he made us aware of the Holy Spirit because the Holy Spirit has always been with us.

In Genesis, it says: the Spirit of God moved over the face of the deep. The Holy Spirit came upon Mary. Elizabeth was filled with the Holy Spirit even before Jesus was born. Jesus, himself, says, "God is spirit, and must be worshipped in Spirit and truth." Even our bodies, according to Paul, are the temple of the Holy Spirit. He preaches God is that in which we live and move and have our being. The Spirit is all around us. We are awash in an ocean of Spirit, but we cannot see it. We swim like fish unaware of the sea. Indeed, we can be blind to the Spirit. That's why there are so many stories of healing blindness in Christian Scripture. Jesus grabs us by our shoulders, turns us around and points to God. There, there, don't you see? But none are so blind as those who will not see.

In Hebrew there is a word, *Ruach*, or the breath of God, the same breath of God that was breathed into Adam's nostrils at creation. The *Ruach*, the breath of God gave Adam life. The words spirit and inspiration and expiration all come from the same Latin root, *spiritus* which can mean both spirit and breath and the verb form, *spirare* means 'to breathe.' Spirit and breath are very closely connected. With inspiration we breathe God in. With expiration, we breathe God out. As the Ruach, the breath of God, gave life to Adam, breathing quite literally gives us life. We truly breathe God in and breathe God out every second of every day. It makes God as close as our breath.

This was the Good News of Jesus: the Kingdom of God is at hand. It is near. It is as close as your breath. The Kingdom of God Jesus preached is not a place where you can say, " 'Look, here it is!' or 'There it is!' For, in fact, the kingdom of God is within you."

We have the breath of the divine within us. We are all a commingling of the spiritual and the material. Both the creator and the created live within us. Richard Rohr says, "We are not human beings trying to be spiritual. We are spiritual beings trying to be human." Even the symbol of our faith, the cross itself, is an intersection of two planes, the vertical or heavenly plane and the horizontal or earthly plane. We live at the intersection of the sacred and the profane. We exist at the crossroads of the eternal and the temporal. Isn't that inconsistent? Well, of course it is. We are walking inconsistencies. We are divinely inspired human paradoxes. The reason Bible stories are inconsistent is because we are inconsistent.

I think I have finally been partially cured of my blindness. I can now see the divine in each of you, the Holy Spirit in each of you, the Christ in each of you. I can now see Christ in my friend, Eyleen Farmer, who ministers to prostitutes with her Thistle and Bee project. I can now see Christ in my friend, Elaine Blanchard, who ministers to prisoners, gays and lesbians and the transgendered just by helping them tell their own stories, and I can now see the Christ in each of you. The Christ in Eyleen, the Christ in Elaine and the Christ in each of you appears to me, appears to me in my own fear-shuttered room, and breathes on me. Christ in you breathes on me and I, once again, receive the Holy Spirit. Thanks be to God, amen.

REST

Now, he was teaching in one of the synagogues on the sabbath. And just then there appeared a woman with a spirit that had crippled her for eighteen years. She was bent over and was quite unable to stand up straight. When Jesus saw her, he called her over and said, "Woman, you are set free from your ailment." When he laid his hands on her, immediately she stood up straight and began praising God. But the leader of the synagogue, indignant because Jesus had cured on the sabbath, kept saying to the crowd, "There are six days on which work ought to be done; come on those days and be cured, and not on the sabbath day." But the Lord answered him and said, "You hypocrites! Does not each of you on the sabbath untie his ox or his donkey from the manger, and lead it away to give it water? And ought not this woman, a daughter of Abraham whom Satan bound for eighteen long years, be set free from this bondage on the sabbath day?" When he said this, all his opponents were put to shame; and the entire crowd was rejoicing at all the wonderful things that he was doing.

Luke 13:10-17

In Walter Brueggemann's book, *Sabbath as Resistance*, he teaches that resting on the Sabbath harkens back to the Exodus. Having escaped from the land of Egypt, he teaches, the Hebrews decided they would never again be slaves like they were in Egypt. To insure it, a day was set aside as a day of rest from labor, the Sabbath Day.

This message of exodus from Egypt is reflected in the Gospel today. Jesus tells the bent woman, "You are *set free* from your ailment." He says, "ought not this woman, a daughter of Abraham (meaning she was a Jew) ought not this Jewish woman, . . . be *set free* from this *bondage*?" On the Sabbath Day we are set free from our labor so we may rest.

Last year, I went to Heber Springs and raced in a triathlon. I was out of shape and barely finished. It took quite a toll on me. Afterwards I had difficulty sitting for any length of time. When I drove or sat at my desk for more than 15 minutes my hamstring would ache terribly. I would have to stand and walk around.

One night I was having dinner with a doctor friend of mine. I said, "Hey, Doc, I've got this pain," and I told him about my poor hamstrings. "What would be your advice for a guy like me." He did not hesitate, but immediately blurted out his one-word prescription. "Rest!" he said. "You need rest." I followed his advice and with a lot of rest and some gentle stretching, I am happy to report, that my hamstrings have greatly improved.

I thought about my doctor friend when I read this Gospel story. The Sabbath give us the freedom to rest, and rest heals us. Isn't it ironic that the indignant leader criticized Jesus for healing people on, of all days, the Sabbath Day, a day set aside for healing rest? The indignant leader by strictly enforcing the fourth commandment, violated it. What an interesting paradox! What a study in contrasts!

I can identify with the people in this story. I too, like the indignant leader, have been blindly obedient to rules to such an extent that I have created the very situation the rule was designed to avoid. Sometimes making an idol out of rules can enslave us to them. They make us rule-bound and pharisaic. They can return us to the land of Egypt.

Yes, I can identify with the people in this story. I, too, like the bent woman, have suffered with a crippling spirit, and I suspect that some of you have too. The crippling spirit of depression, the crippling spirit of addiction, the crippling spirit of ego and pride and superiority, the crippling spirit of fear, the crippling spirit of the loss of a child, the crippling spirit of resentment and anger and jealousy and loneliness and isolation. These things can lay us low. They double us over where we, like the bent woman, are quite unable to stand up straight. It is my prayer today that we receive a Sabbath healing of our crippling spirit. May we be set free from this bondage. May the peace of God lead us out of the slavery of Egypt into the healing freedom of the Promised Land. May the Holy Spirit show us the way into God's Kingdom.   Amen.

THE FOX IS AFOOT

Some Pharisees came and said to Jesus, "Get away from here, for Herod wants to kill you." He said to them, "Go and tell that fox for me, 'Listen, I am casting out demons and performing cures today and tomorrow, and on the third day I finish my work. Yet today, tomorrow, and the next day I must be on my way, because it is impossible for a prophet to be killed outside of Jerusalem.' Jerusalem, Jerusalem, the city that kills the prophets and stones those who are sent to it! How often have I desired to gather your children together as a hen gathers her brood under her wings, and you were not willing! See, your house is left to you. And I tell you, you will not see me until the time comes when you say, 'Blessed is the one who comes in the name of the Lord.'"

Luke 13:31-35

Well, it looks like Herod, once again, wants to kill Jesus. You should know that this is not the same Herod who wanted to kill Jesus when he was an infant. This is not the Herod who caused Jesus' family to flee to Egypt. That was Herod the Great, and he is long dead when this story takes place. No, this is his son, Herod Antipas. Isn't it strange? As soon as you feel safe from one Herod, another Herod, more dangerous than the first, always takes his place.

Jesus' metaphor about hens and foxes is an apt one. Jesus, like a mother hen, is imperiled by that fox, Herod. I have been told when a hen's brood is approached by a fox, the hen will gather her chicks beneath her. She will puff herself up. She will arch her wings to appear as large as she can and then she will turn and face the approaching fox, and even though she is killed, she distracts that fox long enough for her chicks to scurry to safety. This image of sacrifice evokes the story of Christ's sacrifice and through imitation of Christ our own sacrifice for others.

We don't talk about sacrifice, enough. It comes from two Latin words, *sacer,* which means "sacred;" or holy and *facere* which means to make. Sacrifice is derived from the Latin meaning to make holy. I believe Jesus was made holy by his sacrifice, and we too, as we imitate Christ, are made holy by our sacrifices. You see sacrifice is just another word for love.

I was soul sick when I learned that the State of Tennessee, out of fear, was going to deny refuge to vulnerable people fleeing oppression. My God, I thought, the terrorists have won. They have achieved their goal. They have changed our behavior by instilling us with fear. But this gospel story today teaches me that Jesus overcame his fear of a terrorist. Jesus decided he would not flee to Egypt, ever again, out of fear of a terrorist king. You tell that fox for me that I will be right here tending to my people for three days and then I'm going to Jerusalem. And who lives in Jerusalem? The fox does.

In this season of Lent, we try to imitate Christ's experience in the wilderness. We expose ourselves in a small, symbolic way to the wild beasts, to the elements, to hunger, to thirst, to the temptations of the devil, himself, trusting God will send his angels to minister to us as he did Jesus.

And we need God's angels to minister to us because you see being a Christian is not all sweetness and light. The wilderness can be very dangerous place. It has a sharp edge to it. It can expose us to risks and dangers we'd rather not encounter. Accepting refugees into the United States may expose us to risks, but love always does, doesn't it? Love always entails risk and danger because when we love we make ourselves vulnerable just like that mother hen.

There is evil in the world, my friends, that can paralyze us with fear. The question that Christ asks us is how are we going to respond to evil. Are we going to flee to Egypt, yet again, or are we going to follow Christ to Jerusalem? Jesus says be not afraid. He calls us to Jerusalem because that fox, Herod, the terrorist king, may have died, but a new Herod has taken his place. The new terrorist king is alive, and he still wants to kill Christ. The Herod within us still wants to kill the Christ within us.

In times of danger, imitate Christ. When terrorists like Herod fill us with fear, when we are afraid of doing what we know Christ is calling us to do, in this season of Lent, as we contemplate Christ's hardship in the wilderness, let us take comfort in Paul's words of encouragement to the Corinthians: "Be courageous, be strong, stand firm in your faith and in all you do, do it with love." Amen

CHRISTMAS IS OVER

Jesus came from Galilee to John at the Jordan, to be baptized by him. John would have prevented him, saying, "I need to be baptized by you, and do you come to me?" But Jesus answered him, "Let it be so now; for it is proper for us in this way to fulfill all righteousness." Then he consented. And when Jesus had been baptized, just as he came up from the water, suddenly the heavens were opened to him and he saw the Spirit of God descending like a dove and alighting on him. And a voice from heaven said, "This is my Son, the Beloved, with whom I am well pleased."

Mark 3:13-17

Christmas is over. All twelve days of it. We've opened all the presents. We've toasted in the New Year and here we sit in the bleak, midwinter, post-holiday funk. We've enjoyed a lot of time off, and now we have to go back to work. We are getting those thin, rectangular gifts in the mail that contain our credit card statements. And it's getting cold outside. Yes, seasonal effective disorder is beginning to set in, and there is not another holiday until Memorial Day! That's an eon from now! It can be depressing, can't it, in this bleak, midwinter, post-holiday funk time of year.

Have you ever had the experience of everyone around you wishing you a happy new year and you just aren't having one? My favorite comedian, George Carlin, says he hates it when people say to him, "Have a nice day," because that puts all the pressure on him. Now he has to go out and somehow arrange to have a nice day, and, if he doesn't, he feels he has let people down. "They told me to have a nice day and I didn't have one." That's the way I sometimes feel about Happy New Year, especially when I'm not having one.

The Episcopal liturgical calendar has a strange name for this season. It's called Epiphany. I looked up Epiphany in the dictionary and it has nothing to do with a bleak, midwinter, post-holiday funk. It is a sudden, unexpected manifestation of the divine. Traditionally we read the story of the wise men which we did last Sunday and the baptism of Jesus which we've read today. Both stories are epiphanies. The wise men following a star to the Christ child, and the Holy Spirit descending on Jesus as God declares himself pleased.

I kind of associate with John in the story. Why does the king of kings, the alpha and the omega, the prince of peace, the savior of humanity have to be baptized by anyone? It seems like Jesus ought to be doing the baptizing. I want Jesus to change places with John, but it is John who has to take the active role. It is John who does the baptizing. And Jesus replies, "Let it be so now; for it is proper for us in this way to fulfill all righteousness." Of course, I remember from my catechism that baptism is an initiation into the Christian community where we are welcomed into the fellowship of the Spirit.

Last week I was in a post-holiday funk kind of mood so I decided to come to this service. There, I was conscripted to take up the collection. The collection followed the passing of the peace in the service. I passed out a few perfunctory "peaces" and then made a mad dash to the narthex where my usher mate was waiting with the plates. While we were waiting, plates in hand, for our musical cue to walk down the aisle, I noticed a friend of mine, who was sitting in the front of the church, pop up and walk briskly and purposefully to the back of the church. I wondered, "Where is he going? He must have something important to do!" He walked right up to me and stuck his hand out. I shifted the plate to my left and accepted his offered right hand. He said, "May the peace of the Lord be with you, Jack." And then he turned and walked back to his pew as quickly as he had come.

And as if it was waiting on my friend's proclamation, the peace of the Lord was suddenly with me. I felt the Spirit descending on me like a dove. I felt like I had been immersed in the River Jordan and had emerged fresh and new again. I almost heard a faint voice calling out to me. I was no longer in a post-holiday funk. It was an epiphany. It was a sudden and unexpected manifestation of the Holy.

And so, in this season of Epiphany, let us take the active role, like the Three Wise Men did, by searching the heavens for that star that can guide us to Bethlehem. You see Bethlehem is not a town in the Middle East. It is a place in the human heart where Christ is born, all year long. May we take an active role in our own salvation, like John did, by constantly looking for an approaching Christ asking us to baptize him. May we, like John, take the active role by baptizing him into our community, by initiating his ministry of peace into or hearts and lives. For as he said, "Let it be so now; for it is proper for us in this way to fulfill all righteousness."

In this bleak midwinter, post-holiday funk season, I will take the active role and leave you with the same words my friend left with me that Sunday. May the peace of the Lord be with **you**.

Oh, and Happy New Year, and, by all means, . . . have a nice day!

TRANSFIGURATION

Six days later, Jesus took with him Peter and James and his brother John and led them up a high mountain, by themselves. And he was transfigured before them, and his face shone like the sun, and his clothes became dazzling white. Suddenly there appeared to them Moses and Elijah, talking with him. Then Peter said to Jesus, "Lord, it is good for us to be here; if you wish, I will make three dwellings here, one for you, one for Moses, and one for Elijah." While he was still speaking, suddenly a bright cloud overshadowed them, and from the cloud a voice said, "This is my Son, the Beloved; with him I am well pleased; listen to him!" When the disciples heard this, they fell to the ground and were overcome by fear. But Jesus came and touched them, saying, "Get up and do not be afraid." And when they looked up, they saw no one except Jesus himself alone.

Matthew 17:1-9

Well, here we are on the last Sunday after Epiphany. Lent starts on Wednesday. But now, it is still the season of Epiphany, Epiphany which is defined as a sudden, unexpected encounter with the divine, a theophany as it is sometimes called. All through Epiphany we have been reading stories of divine encounters from the Three Wise Men and their guiding star, to the presentation of Jesus in the Temple, to the Baptism of Jesus and the divine voice proclaiming Jesus' sonship and God's pleasure. And today, the Last Sunday in Epiphany, the season of Epiphany culminates in the story of the Transfiguration, where Jesus, James, John and Peter climb the Holy Mountain. Jesus converses with Moses and Elijah and his face and clothing shine with God's Glory. Once again God's voice is heard, "This is my son in whom I am well pleased" the exact words spoken at Jesus' baptism with the added admonition, "Listen to him." The story is an epiphany. It is a theophany. It is a sudden and unexpected encounter with the divine. I suspect that encounter was much more sudden and much more unexpected for James, John and Peter than it was for Jesus. Certainly, Jesus knew more than they what was about to happen. It was more of an epiphany for James, John and Peter than it was for him.

I sometimes wonder: just exactly who is being transfigured here. I know. I know! It is the story about the transfiguration of Jesus, but I've learned that some early church fathers wrote that while Jesus was, indeed, transfigured, James and John and Peter were transfigured as well. They call it the Transfiguration of the Believer for you see it is really James and John and Peter who were transformed by their ascent up that mountain. Their perception of Jesus was changed. They, literally, now see Jesus in a new light. They are able to see the light of God shining through Jesus. They can finally hear the voice of God calling to them. Perhaps the Story of the Transfiguration is more about James, John and Peter than it is about Jesus. I like that interpretation because if the story is about the transformation of the followers of Jesus maybe other followers of Jesus who were born two thousand years later can be transfigured, too, people like you and me. That makes the story of the Transfiguration a story about us. We are in the story. It is not a story about people who lived long ago, far, far away. It is about the here and now. It is a story that reoccurs every day and every place. It is unfolding right here in Memphis, Tennessee. The plot of the story of the Transfiguration is developing right now at the Church of the Holy Communion. When we tell the story, we can just as easily substitute the names of James, John, and Peter with our own names or the names of the people in the pews next to you.

Maybe you and I, with our brother, Christ, as our guide, can climb that Holy Mountain and finally see the glory of God shining through Christ *and through other people*. Maybe we can be changed so that we, too, can finally hear God's voice calling to us, so that we too can experience epiphany and be transfigured.

TRANSFIGURATION REDUX

Jesus took with him Peter and James and John, and led them up a high mountain apart, by themselves. And he was transfigured before them, and his clothes became dazzling white, such as no one on earth could bleach them. And there appeared to them Elijah with Moses, who were talking with Jesus. Then Peter said to Jesus, "Rabbi, it is good for us to be here; let us make three dwellings, one for you, one for Moses, and one for Elijah." He did not know what to say, for they were terrified. Then a cloud overshadowed them, and from the cloud there came a voice, "This is my Son, the Beloved; listen to him!" Suddenly when they looked around, they saw no one with them any more, but only Jesus. As they were coming down the mountain, he ordered them to tell no one about what they had seen, until after the Son of Man had risen from the dead.

Mark 9:2-9

I have written about the story of the transfiguration. Specifically, I have written about the transfiguration of the believer, how it was not just Jesus who was transfigured on top of the holy mountain, but how James and John and Peter were transfigured there as well because now they quite literally saw Jesus in a new light. Now they were able to see the glory of God shining through Jesus. Now they could finally hear the voice of God saying "listen to him!" They were changed by that experience. They were transfigured on top of the holy mountain with Christ and by implication we too are transfigured with Christ. This is the story of the transfiguration of the believer by the glory of God shining through Jesus.

I love the 5:30 service at the Church of the Holy Communion. It transfigures me. It is filled with the glory of God in the holy silence, in the sacred chants. It can take me to heights of joy and depths of weeping in the span of seconds in the giving and receiving of the sacrament, in the passing of the peace, in the blessing of the priest. These things transfigure me. I don't want to leave. I want to build three dwelling places, one for Jesus, one for Moses and one for Elijah and maybe a little one for me. I want to stay on top of the holy mountain. But I can't. I have to descend from the holy mountain and engage with the world and, my friends, it can be a cold, dark, broken world, a world broken by addiction, disease, depression and loneliness, a broken world where a family in North Carolina is executed over a parking dispute, a broken world where a 15-year-old boy bludgeons a refugee over a dinged car door, a broken world where we are fighting never-ending, worldwide wars. What are we to do? How do we respond? What is a Christian to do in such a broken world?

I love the evening service at Holy Communion and I am coming to realize the holiest moment of it, the most sacred part of the service is after the silence, after the reflection, after the blessing of the priest, when the music stops . . . . and we quietly gather up our things and slowly move into the darkness. Like human candles, like tiny specks of light filled with the Holy Spirit we get into our cars and drive into the night. I believe that God really did transfigure Jesus who in turn transfigured James and John and Peter and you and me. There is a glory within us that transfigures us if we awake to it.

You and I have ascended to the top of the holy mountain with Christ. You and I have seen Jesus transfigured by God's glory and you and I, in turn, have been transfigured by the glory of God's love shining through Jesus. Now, you and I must descend from the holy mountain with Christ. You and I must leave this place. Shining with the God's glory, you and I must walk into that cold, dark, broken night and transfigure the world . . .transfigure the world.

TRINITY SUNDAY

The eleven disciples went to Galilee, to the mountain to which Jesus had directed them. When they saw him, they worshiped him; but some doubted. And Jesus came and said to them, "All authority in heaven and on earth has been given to me. Go therefore and make disciples of all nations, baptizing them in the name of the Father and of the Son and of the Holy Spirit, and teaching them to obey everything that I have commanded you. And remember, I am with you always, to the end of the age."

Matthew 28:16-20

Today is Trinity Sunday. The Gospel reading today is The Great Commission. It is generally read on Trinity Sunday because in it Jesus says, "Go therefore and make disciples of all nations, baptizing them in the name of the Father and of the Son and of the Holy Spirit."

My favorite gospel is John's Gospel. In it Jesus says I am in the Father and the Father is in me. But he doesn't stop there. He continues: And you are in me, and I am in you.

So, If we are in Christ and Christ is in the Father maybe we can think of the Trinity as a set of concentric circles or spheres. We start with you and me. We are contained inside the first circle which is Christ. The second circle is God the Father. We are in Christ and Christ, the first circle, is in the Father, the second circle. This fits nicely with Paul's statement that we are living members of the body of Christ. This fits even better with Paul's statement that God is that in which we live and move and have our being.

My favorite Bible verse is 1 John 4:16, "God is love and those who abide in love abide in God and God abides in them." Abiding in God also fits in the circle metaphor. Thomas Cramner, the Archbishop of Canterbury in the 16th century, wrote many of the collects in the Book of Common Prayer. He ends many saying we pray to God the Father through his son Jesus who both live and reign together in the unity of the Holy Spirit. So, we are in Christ, who is in God, both of whom live and reign together in the unity of the Holy Spirit, the third circle. So, we have three concentric circles, Christ, God the Father both of whom live and reign in the unity of the third circle, the Holy Spirit. And these circles are not static. They move in and out and are encapsulated by each other. They are dynamic. They radiate and pulsate.

Thinking of the Trinity as concentric circles is not new. It goes back to the 4th century. St. Hilary of Poitiers came up with a model of the Trinity in which each person of the Trinity reciprocally contains each other person of the Trinity at the same time so that each permanently envelopes and is permanently enveloped by each of the others simultaneously. It even has a name. It is called Perichoresis or Circumcessio. Like an electron that is at every location around its nucleus, so each person of the Trinity contains and is contained by each other person of the Trinity at every moment in time according to Perichoresis

Thinking of God as circular or spherical is not limited to our culture. Other beliefs find the divine in circles. Black Elk was a Lakota Native American Medicine Man who lived in the latter part of the 19th century. He says that the circle is a sacred symbol. To Native Americans everything is a circle, the sun, the moon, the stars, a tree's trunk. The very horizon is a circle. For Black Elk, Native Americans lost their power when white men forced them live in square houses.

St. Augustine is credited with saying, "God is a circle, the center of which is everywhere and the circumference of which is nowhere."

Edwin Markham wrote a poem called "Outwitted." "He drew a circle that shut me out, heretic, rebel, a thing to flout, but Love and I had the wit to win. We drew a circle and took him in."

Henry of Poitiers, Black Elk, Thomas Cramner, Augustine, and Edwin Markham would all agree that we are contained within sacred circles. While we might live in square houses, we abide, as John so ably put it, we abide in sacred circles.

This we pray to God the Father through God the Son who both live and reign together in the unity of the Holy Spirit. Amen

WHO DO PEOPLE
SAY THAT I AM?

When Jesus came into the district of Caesarea Philippi, he asked his disciples, "Who do people say that the Son of Man is?" And they said, "Some say John the Baptist, but others Elijah, and still others Jeremiah or one of the prophets." He said to them, "But who do you say that I am?" Simon Peter answered, "You are the Messiah, the Son of the living God." And Jesus answered him, "Blessed are you, Simon son of Jonah! For flesh and blood has not revealed this to you, but my Father in heaven. And I tell you, you are Peter, and on this rock, I will build my church, and the gates of Hades will not prevail against it. I will give you the keys of the kingdom of heaven, and whatever you bind on earth will be bound in heaven, and whatever you loose on earth will be loosed in heaven." Then he sternly ordered the disciples not to tell anyone that he was the Messiah.

Matthew 16:13-20

Who do people say that the Son of Man is? That is a question that has been asked by a lot by people down through the ages. Unlike Mark's version, Matthew has Jesus refer to himself as the Son of Man. Just what does Jesus mean when he refers to himself as the Son of Man? I have read that it is a reference to Jesus's humanity. When Jesus talks about himself in human terms, being a human myself, I can relate much better.

We did not read the epistle assigned for today. I wonder if these gospel readings are paired with an epistle for a reason or if they are coupled together haphazardly. I think that it is done for a reason. In today's epistle Paul writes, "For as in one body we have many members, and not all the members have the same function, so we, who are many, are one body in Christ, and individually we are members one of another."

In First Corinthians, Paul also refers to the body. He says, "Now you are the body of Christ and severally members thereof." Jesus says to his disciples in John's gospel, "Whoever believes in me will do the works I have been doing, and they will do even greater things than these." All of these Bible verses point to our affinity and likeness to the person of Jesus and the spirit of Christ.

Indeed, we are in Christ and Christ is in us. Holy Communion is a symbolic way of commemorating how we have incorporated into ourselves the elements of the Christ. The prayer after communion says it well. "Now send us forth a people forgiven, healed, renewed, that we may proclaim your love to the world and continue in the risen life of Christ our savior." It is we who continue the risen life of Christ. In fact, the name, "Christian" was given to the early followers of Jesus because it means "little Christ."

I have met many Christ-like people who have both redeemed and saved me. I have seen Christ in these people. One of them was my brother-in-law, Duane Saba. He was the associate rector here years ago under Eric Greenwood until he took over a parish in Helena, Arkansas. He loved being a priest. He would tell my sister, "I don't know why they pay me for doing this." When he died the headline read, "Christ-like Priest dies in Helena, Arkansas." I believe that we as humans have the potential to be Christ-like. We have the potential to be messiahs with a small "m" and saviors with a small "s" to one another. Christ is just the Greek word for "anointed one of God." We, too, have been anointed by God in many ways. We have been anointed by God with our lives, with our intellect, with our capacity to love and be loved. Our very existence attests to it, and as we grow in the image and likeness of God we can become co-heirs with Christ, our brother, of God's spirit. We can with Christ's example become sons and daughters of the living God.

And so, the question is not about Jesus, is it? It is about you and me. Perhaps we should be asking, "Who do people say that *you* are? Who do people say that *we* are?"

FOLLOW ME

After John was arrested, Jesus came to Galilee, proclaiming the good news of God, and saying, "The time is fulfilled, and the kingdom of God has come near; repent, and believe in the good news."

As Jesus passed along the Sea of Galilee, he saw Simon and his brother Andrew casting a net into the sea—for they were fishermen. And Jesus said to them, "Follow me and I will make you fish for people." And immediately they left their nets and followed him. As he went a little farther, he saw James son of Zebedee and his brother John, who were in their boat mending the nets. Immediately he called them; and they left their father Zebedee in the boat with the hired men, and followed him.

Mark 1:14-20

I was taught that the word, "Gospel," means "Good News," but I have often wondered just exactly what is this good news that Jesus is always talking about.

Our lesson for today sheds some light on the issue. Mark says, "Now after John was arrested, Jesus came to Galilee, proclaiming the good news of God, and saying, ..." Uh oh! Wait a minute. Better pay attention here, because it looks like Jesus is just about to tell me what this Good News is!

Mark continues, ". . . and saying 'The time is fulfilled, and the kingdom of God has come near; repent, and believe in the good news.'" Wait. Is Jesus saying that the Good News is that the Kingdom of God has come near? What does that mean?

Well, we know that in the Hebrew Scripture, God was unapproachable. He was always on a mountaintop where even Moses only saw his back side as he moved away from him, or he was hidden away in the Arc of the Covenant or shrouded behind the veil in the Holy of Holies where only the High Priest could go once a year. Jesus has good news, and that news is revolutionary. The Kingdom of God is not on a mountaintop. It is not enshrouded in the Holy of Holies. The Kingdom of God is near and available to us all.

But just how do we get to this nearby Kingdom of God? That brings us to the second part of this story. I find it extremely interesting that the proclamation of the nearness of the Kingdom of God is placed in such close proximity to Jesus calling his disciples to follow him. It is almost as if he is saying the Kingdom of God is near, and I know where it is. I will show you the way. Come and follow me to this nearby kingdom.

I've been reading a book called the *Restoration Project* by Christopher Martin. In it he says Jesus has a whole lot of admirers. Jesus' admirers are all over the place, commonplace, in fact. Jesus has so many admirers that he really doesn't need any more admirers. What Jesus needs are not admirers, but followers, followers. So, what does it mean to follow Jesus?

Paul writes how we must go to the Holy City of Jerusalem with

Christ, we must pray with Christ in the Garden of Gethsemane, we must obey God's will for us, as Christ did. We must confront the Temple authorities with Christ, we must be crucified with Christ, we must be raised with Christ by dying to one way of being and resurrected into another way of being as a new creation. We must die to our ego and be resurrected into community. We must die to our addictions and be resurrected into recovery. We must die to our fears and be resurrected into love. In following Jesus, and obeying God's will for us, we are spiritually transformed. We undergo a spiritual awakening. We enter the Kingdom that Jesus speaks of. In short, we are saved.

Most of the time, it is a long, slow, steady trudge into the Holy City, but at every turn in the road on our way we catch quick glimpses of the Christ of Faith, just ahead, beckoning to us, only to quickly disappear again around the next bend. We struggle to keep up, but with that wee, small voice within, he calls us just as he called Simon and Andrew and James and John. He calls to us just as he calls a priest to ordination. He calls to us, not in Galilee 2000 years ago, but right here, right now. I have good news, he says. The Kingdom of God is near, he says. I know where it is; I will show you the way, he says.

Come. Follow me.

Follow me.

THE TEST

J esus said, "When the Son of Man comes in his glory, and all
the angels with him, then he will sit on the throne of his glory.
All the nations will be gathered before him, and he will separate people one from another as a shepherd separates the sheep
from the goats, and he will put the sheep at his right hand and the
goats at the left. Then the king will say to those at his right hand,
'Come, you that are blessed by my Father, inherit the kingdom prepared for you from the foundation of the world; for I was hungry
and you gave me food, I was thirsty and you gave me something
to drink, I was a stranger and you welcomed me, I was naked and
you gave me clothing, I was sick and you took care of me, I was in
prison and you visited me.' Then the righteous will answer him,
'Lord, when was it that we saw you hungry and gave you food, or
thirsty and gave you something to drink? And when was it that
we saw you a stranger and welcomed you, or naked and gave you
clothing? And when was it that we saw you sick or in prison and
visited you?' And the king will answer them, 'Truly I tell you, just
as you did it to one of the least of these who are members of my
family, you did it to me.' Then he will say to those at his left hand,
'You that are accursed, depart from me into the eternal fire prepared for the devil and his angels; for I was hungry and you gave
me no food, I was thirsty and you gave me nothing to drink, I was a
stranger and you did not welcome me, naked and you did not give
me clothing, sick and in prison and you did not visit me.' Then
they also will answer, 'Lord, when was it that we saw you hungry
or thirsty or a stranger or naked or sick or in prison, and did not
take care of you?' Then he will answer them, 'Truly I tell you, just
as you did not do it to one of the least of these, you did not do it
to me.' And these will go away into eternal punishment, but the

righteous into eternal life."

Matthew 25:31-46

A minister once told me, based on Matthew's parable of the Sheep and the Goats, that when he is approached by a panhandler, he thinks to himself, "This may not be a panhandler. This may be Christ the Lord, disguised as a panhandler, and this . . . this is a test."

I have a friend who buys meals for panhandlers rather than giving them money. He tells the story of how he was approached outside a McDonalds by a homeless man who asked if had any spare change. My friend said, "I won't give you any money, but I will buy you a meal at this McDonald's." The man said, "I . . . I . . . I don't like the food here." My friend said, "Well that's what I can do for you."

"Oh, all right," he said and my friend bought him a Big Mac, french fries and a coke, and after that encounter, my friend said he felt strangely blessed by the experience.

Years ago, I was asked to coach a pee-wee football team. I didn't know much about football but I guess I knew more than a twelve-year-old. So, I agreed. As I grew to know the kids and developed a relationship with the boys most of whom were poor, African Americans, I felt they taught me much more than I could ever teach them.

I have another friend who goes to a Soup Kitchen with his grown son who is a cook. His son likes to prepare the food, but my friend likes to greet people at the door, shake their hands, bring them food and drink, look into their eyes. He says when he does, he comes away feeling blessed by the experience.

My wife and I adopted a dog a couple of years ago. His name is Barkley. He's a rescue dog and that dog is the most affectionate dog I have ever had. He is constantly following me around; he sits at my feet; he whines all day until I get home. I have a theory that rescue dogs are affectionate because they know what it's like out on the streets alone. They really appreciate a warm, dry bed and a full belly. Barkley has had a huge impact on our lives. We have fallen in love with Barkley, and he loves us. My wife likes to say, "Yes, he is a rescue dog, all right, but just exactly who is rescuing whom, here?"

In a just a few moments we are going to pray the Lord's Prayer together, again. We will pray as Jesus taught us. "Forgive us our trespasses as we forgive those who trespass against us."

Maybe when we feed other people it is we who are being fed. When we teach other people, it is we who are taught, when we serve other people, it is we who are being served, when we forgive others, we are forgiven, when we rescue other people, or dogs, it is we who are being rescued. Maybe that's what the Bible means when it says we recognize Christ in the breaking of the bread. Maybe THIS is exactly how Jesus saves us, through the least of these.

Mother Theresa once said, "My work is done for, with and TO Jesus. We serve HIM in the neighbor, we see HIM in the poor, nurse HIM in the sick, we comfort HIM in his afflicted brothers and sisters. "

So maybe my minister friend had it right. Maybe that panhandler really is Christ the Lord and this . . . this is a test.

GOOD FRIDAY

When Jesus then saw His mother, and the disciple whom He loved standing nearby, He said to His mother, "Woman, behold, your son!" Then He said to the disciple, "Behold, your mother!" From that hour the disciple took her into his own household.

John 19:26-27

Who, exactly, is this disciple whom Jesus loved? Most people say it was John because it's in his Gospel, but this disciple whom Jesus loved is unnamed. Didn't Jesus love all of his disciples? Didn't he say, "I give you a new commandment to love one another as I have loved you?" I like to think that the unnamed disciple whom Jesus loved could be any of his disciples, even his present-day disciples. That would include you and me. We might easily insert our names in place of the words, the disciple whom Jesus loved. You see, it is you and I standing there at the foot of the cross next to Mary looking up at our dying savior and hearing him say to Mary, "Woman, behold your son," referring to us and since in Christ there is no male or female, the words could easily be, "Woman, behold your daughter." He then turns to us, the disciple whom Jesus loves, and he says to us, "Behold your mother." And from that hour we take her into our own household. Jesus' mother is now our mother.

Mary has been called the Universal Mother, the new Eve. Not the old Eve, who stumbled and fell in the garden but the new Eve, Mary, who now becomes the spiritual mother of all of us. She gave a physical birth to Jesus who gives a spiritual rebirth to us.

Remember earlier in John's Gospel when Jesus tells Nicodemus you must be born again? We must be born of the Spirit, he says. Jesus was certainly born of the Spirit. If we are Jesus' disciples, the one whom Jesus loves, then we, too, must be born of the Spirit. Jesus' spiritual father is our father. Jesus' mother is our mother. We share common parentage with Christ. We become members of the immediate family of Christ. We now see that Jesus is truly our elder brother. We must take our brother's place in the world by becoming the hands and feet of Christ, to assume our position as a member of the mystical body of Christ and continue in the life of our risen Lord.

Who, exactly, is this disciple whom Jesus loved?

REAPPROPRIATION

The crowd came together again, so that Jesus and his disciples could not even eat. When his family heard it, they went out to restrain him, for people were saying, "He has gone out of his mind." And the scribes who came down from Jerusalem said, "He has Beelzebub, and by the ruler of the demons he casts out demons." And he called them to him, and spoke to them in parables, "How can Satan cast out Satan? If a kingdom is divided against itself, that kingdom cannot stand. And if a house is divided against itself, that house will not be able to stand. And if Satan has risen up against himself and is divided, he cannot stand, but his end has come. But no one can enter a strong man's house and plunder his property without first tying up the strong man; then indeed the house can be plundered.

"Truly I tell you, people will be forgiven for their sins and whatever blasphemies they utter; but whoever blasphemes against the Holy Spirit can never have forgiveness, but is guilty of an eternal sin"— for they had said, "He has an unclean Spirit."

Then his mother and his brothers came; and standing outside, they sent to him and called him. A crowd was sitting around him; and they said to him, "Your mother and your brothers and sisters are outside, asking for you." And he replied, "Who are my mother and my brothers?" And looking at those who sat around him, he said, "Here are my mother and my brothers! Whoever does the will of God is my brother and sister and mother."

Mark 3:20-35

There are many words in our lexicon that started out as insults but later were adopted by the very people being insulted. One of these words is the word "gay." It was originally given a derisive meaning, but it is now accepted by the very group it derided. Did you know that the words Methodist and Unitarian began as insults but were later adopted by those groups? A Hoosier was an uneducated hayseed but now Indianans proudly refer to themselves by that term, and even Merle Haggard is proud to be an "Okie" from Muskogee.

This process of changing a word from an insult to a source of pride is called reappropriation. I thought about reappropriation when I read today's gospel. Jesus' family hurries to him because they were told he was out of his mind. Something's wrong with Jesus. He's gone crazy! He's out of his mind.

What a compliment! What high praise! We should all be as out of our minds as Jesus was thought to be! We should reappropriate the insult aimed at Jesus. Indeed, Jesus was out of his mind and into his heart, the world of the Spirit. Now don't get me wrong the mind is a wonderful thing. Reason is a gift of the Holy Spirit, but you cannot dissect love and reduce it to its elemental parts through the use of reason. Our minds can take us part of the way but we need our hearts to complete the journey. The prose of reason needs the poetry of the Spirit to make us whole, complete human beings. May the Holy Spirit lead us out of our minds and into our hearts so that we too can cast out demons.

I used to deride people who believed in demons. Only ignorant people believed in demons. Imagine my surprise when I learned I was the ignorant one. I have come to believe in demons, and the reason I have is because I have had to confront several demons in my own life, and I would wager you have too. If you haven't, you will. Demons like excessive ego. Demons like addiction. Demons like anger, demons like greed, demons like failing health, demons like lost relationships, demons like loneliness, demons like fear. These demons can shut out the sunlight of the Spirit. They separate us from God. They must be cast out, but Satan cannot cast out Satan. As Martin Luther King once said, "Darkness will never. . . .cast out darkness." Only light can do that. Only the Spirit can cast out darkness if we are open to it. As John's Epistle has taught us, "There is no fear in love, for perfect love casts out fear."

Harry Meserve wrote a prayer of confession that confronts and casts out modern-day demons. He prays:

> From arrogance, pompousness, and thinking ourselves more important than we are, may some saving sense of humor liberate us.

> For allowing ourselves to ridicule the faith of others, may we be forgiven.

> For making war and calling it peace, indifference and calling it tolerance, pollution and calling it progress, may we be cured.

> For telling ourselves and others that evil is inevitable while good is impossible, may we stand corrected.

> God of our mixed up, tragic, aspiring, doubting, and insurgent lives, help us to be as good in our hearts as we have always wanted to be.

Today may we pray: "Holy Spirit, lead us out of our minds and into our hearts where love resides where the Spirit dwells so that we, too, can cast out demons."

PROPINQUITY

The apostles gathered around Jesus, and told him all that they had done and taught. He said to them, "Come away to a deserted place all by yourselves and rest a while." For many were coming and going, and they had no leisure even to eat. And they went away in the boat to a deserted place by themselves. Now many saw them going and recognized them, and they hurried there on foot from all the towns and arrived ahead of them. As he went ashore, he saw a great crowd; and he had compassion for them, because they were like sheep without a shepherd; and he began to teach them many things.

When they had crossed over, they came to land at Gennesaret and moored the boat. When they got out of the boat, people at once recognized him, and rushed about that whole region and began to bring the sick on mats to wherever they heard he was. And wherever he went, into villages or cities or farms, they laid the sick in the marketplaces, and begged him that they might touch even the fringe of his cloak; and all who touched it were healed.

Mark 6:30-34, 53-56

Propinquity. . . . propinquity. Zelda Gilroy taught me that word. She was a character in a situation comedy that ran in the late 50s and early 60s called "The Many Loves of Dobie Gillis." Zelda was in love with Dobie, and every time Dobie turned a corner, there was Zelda. He would tell her to leave and walk away and immediately run into her again. Why are you following me? Zelda would just smile and say, "Propinquity."

Zelda explained that propinquity is the state of being near, being in close proximity. Zelda's theory was that if she were in close proximity to Dobie, he would fall in love with her. After that, every time Dobie saw Zelda, she would just smile and say, "Propinquity."

I was thinking about Zelda and propinquity when I read today's Gospel. The people at Gennesaret wanted to be near Jesus, they strained to come in close proximity with him, they reached out to touch the fringe of his cloak so they could be healed. They wanted propinquity with Christ.

You and I, unlike the people at Gennesaret, cannot approach the Jesus who walked in first century Palestine. He is gone, but we have the Holy Spirit which came as fire and wind on the day of Pentecost, the very season we are in right now.

Although the man Jesus is physically gone, he is spiritually present because he has given us a helper in the form of the Holy Spirit to comfort us during our times of trial. Sometimes, the Holy Spirit can seem very far off. Indeed, we can, if we choose, banish the Spirit. Deaths, tragedies, our doubts, our fears can separate us from the Spirit. We must work, like the people of Gennesaret worked, to establish propinquity with the Holy Spirit, to come near to the Christ so we, too, can be healed.

Early in Mark's Gospel, he says Jesus began preaching the Good News and saying, "the Kingdom of God is at hand!" It is near, right here, not far.

Propinquity.

In the Hebrew Scripture, God is always on a mountaintop. Only Moses can ascend the mountain to speak to God. But Jesus has taken God off the mountaintop and put him right square in the human heart.

Propinquity.

Yes, sometimes we lose sight of the Spirit. When terrible things happen like the tragic shooting of servicemen in Chattanooga last week. We scream, "Where is God, where is God in all this." Christ might respond, "Look for me. I am there. You might see me in the faces of those who grieve."

Let the Spirit speak to you even in tragedy, especially in tragedy. Perhaps, it will call upon you to comfort those who mourn. Perhaps, it will motivate you to take action so tragedies like this don't happen again.

The Holy Spirit was in Millington, Tennessee this morning, this Eighth Sunday after Pentecost. I read in the paper today about a black church and a white church in Millington reaching out to each other to have joint worship. "We thought because of the incident in Charleston, South Carolina that we would come together," said Pastor Anthony Sledge.

Propinquity.

Walt Whitman wrote:

"If you want me again look for me under your bootsoles.
You will hardly know who I am or what I mean,
But I shall be good help to you nevertheless
And filter and fiber your blood.
Failing to fetch me at first / keep encouraged,
Missing me one place / search another,
I stop some where / waiting for you"

Whitman could be talking about the Holy Spirit. We need to look for the Spirit in our lives and each other's lives even if it seems to be hiding from us, because it is there and has been all along. You'll find it in Chattanooga, Tennessee, in Millington, Tennessee, in Charleston, South Carolina. Look for it here. Look for it now because it is right here, right now, under your bootsoles. Let it filter and fiber your blood. It has stopped some where waiting for you. And when you find it, reach out like the people of Gennesaret, touch the fringe of its cloak and be healed.

Propinquity.

Propinquity.

THE WEDDING
AT CANA

On the third day there was a wedding in Cana of Galilee, and the mother of Jesus was there. Jesus and his disciples had also been invited to the wedding. When the wine gave out, the mother of Jesus said to him, "They have no wine." And Jesus said to her, "Woman, what concern is that to you and to me? My hour has not yet come." His mother said to the servants, "Do whatever he tells you." Now standing there were six stone water jars for the Jewish rites of purification, each holding twenty or thirty gallons. Jesus said to them, "Fill the jars with water." And they filled them up to the brim. He said to them, "Now draw some out, and take it to the chief steward." So, they took it. When the steward tasted the water that had become wine, and did not know where it came from (though the servants who had drawn the water knew), the steward called the bridegroom and said to him, "Everyone serves the good wine first, and then the inferior wine after the guests have become drunk. But you have kept the good wine until now." Jesus did this, the first of his signs, in Cana of Galilee, and revealed his glory; and his disciples believed in him.

John 2:1-11

I have to confess that when I first read the story of the Wedding at Cana, I was not impressed. The story only appears in John's Gospel, but Christians traditionally hold that this is Jesus' very first recorded miracle. It's a trivial miracle as miracles go. I am sure there were things more worthy of Jesus' talents than replenishing the wine at a wedding. One biblical scholar, Michael Homan, claims that word, wine, was mistranslated and that the better word would be "beer." So, does that mean that Jesus' very first miracle was some sort of cosmic, mystical beer run?

I would have expected a much more momentous miracle than that for Jesus' very first miracle. Wouldn't you? Well, perhaps I'm missing something. Maybe, I have taken the story too literally and failed to see some deeper, underlying meaning because there's got to be more to this story than that.

The Wedding at Cana has been the subject of great works of art. There are many Renaissance paintings depicting it, but my favorite work of art about the Wedding at Cana is a country music song written in 1998 by T. Graham Brown called "Wine into Water." When he wrote it, he was in the depths of his alcoholism. It is when I heard the lyrics to Brown's song that my ideas about the wedding at Cana began to change. Brown reverses John's story. The song goes like this (and don't worry, I am not going to sing it):

> Tonight, I'm as low as any man can go
> I'm down and I can't fall much farther
> And once upon a time, You turned the water into wine
> And now, on my knees, I'm turning to You, Father
> Could You help me turn the wine back into water?

Brown's lyrics are more petitionary prayer than song. Of course, Brown is not asking God to physically change wine into water. No, Brown is asking God to change him, to transform him. He is asking that God's spirit enter him so that he may be transfigured. It is not about getting T. Graham Brown into heaven. It is about getting heaven into T. Graham Brown, and I am pleased to report that God answered Brown's prayer. He did change the wine back into water. Brown is sober today.

When I read Bible stories like the one today, I try to identify with one of the characters in the story. That puts me in the story. I can step inside the story and walk around inside the story and see things in the story, I never would have noticed before. It becomes a story about me. It's not about somebody else in a faraway land, long, long ago. It is about me and it is happening here and now.
So, who am I in the Wedding at Cana? Can I identify with Jesus? No, not really. What about Mary? Am I Mary? Nope. Could I be one of the servants or the steward or the bridegroom? Nope, none of those worked for me.

And then it hit me. It hit me like a ton of bricks. I knew who I was in the story. I was not Jesus, or Mary, or the servants, or the steward, or the bridegroom. I was none of those. No, I was the water. You and I are the water, and we are being miraculously transformed into wine, and not just any wine, but the best wine. You and I are being transformed by the Christ into holy wine. For me if Christianity could be reduced to one sentence it would be about individual transformation through the inspiration or incarnation of the Holy Spirit. The Wedding at Cana is not some cosmic, mystical beer run. It is a story about you and me. It is a story about individual transformation through the inspiration of the Holy Spirit. It worked for T. Graham Brown. It can work for us. Amen.

REFUGEES

After the wise men had left, an angel of the Lord appeared to Joseph in a dream and said, "Get up, take the child and his mother, and flee to Egypt, and remain there until I tell you; for Herod is about to search for the child, to destroy him." Then Joseph got up, took the child and his mother by night, and went to Egypt, and remained there until the death of Herod. This was to fulfill what had been spoken by the Lord through the prophet, "Out of Egypt I have called my son."

When Herod died, an angel of the Lord suddenly appeared in a dream to Joseph in Egypt and said, "Get up, take the child and his mother, and go to the land of Israel, for those who were seeking the child's life are dead." Then Joseph got up, took the child and his mother, and went to the land of Israel. But when he heard that Archelaus was ruling over Judea in place of his father Herod, he was afraid to go there. And after being warned in a dream, he went away to the district of Galilee. There he made his home in a town called Nazareth, so that what had been spoken through the prophets might be fulfilled, "He will be called a Nazorean."

Matthew 2:13-15,19-23

T hese Christmas season Gospel stories have made four things clear about Jesus and his family. First, Jesus and his family were very poor. Second, Jesus and his family were homeless. Third, Jesus and his family, as the Gospel for today illustrates, were refugees, and fourth, the richest, most powerful person in all Judea, King Herod, was afraid of them. A rich, powerful man was afraid of poor, homeless, refugees. Things haven't changed much in 2000 years, have they?

Yes, Herod was full of fear and anger, Sometimes it seems there is a lot of fear and anger in our world, too. Every time you turn on the TV or pick up a newspaper there are stories of fear and anger. Some of that fear and anger is directed at poor, homeless, refugees like Jesus and his family. At times, our own fear and anger, the Herod within us, can banish the Holy Spirit to the land of Egypt. Maybe that is why scripture teaches not fear, but the opposite of fear, though the opposite of fear is certainly not courage. No, the opposite of fear is love.

John in his first epistle says, "There is no fear in love, for perfect love casts out fear, . . ." John also says, "God is Love." Christ told us, "I give unto you a new commandment to love one another as I have loved you," because you see If we love one another, the Herod within us dies, and the Holy Spirit can safely return to us from the land of Egypt.

Perhaps, on the Spirit's return, it will teach us that Jesus, himself, was a poor, homeless, refugee. Perhaps the Spirit will help us SEE Christ in ALL poor, homeless refugees.

You see one day, we will say, "Lord, when was it that we saw you hungry and gave you food, or thirsty and gave you something to drink? And when was it that we saw you a stranger and welcomed you, or naked and gave you clothing? And when was it that we saw you sick or in prison and visited you?" And he will say to us, "Just as you did it to one of the least of these my brothers and sisters, you did it to me." Do not be afraid of refugees. Rather, see Christ in them because Christ is there calling to us.

I can hear you saying, "But what can I do about the world refugee problem?" There are plenty of groups that help with refugees. World Relief helps resettle refugees. Perhaps we could volunteer to help them or donate to their cause. World Relief is transforming lives and if we help them in that transformation, do not be surprised if we are not transformed in the process.

Edward Everett Hale once said, " I am only one, but still, I am one. I cannot do everything, but still, I can do something and because I cannot do everything, I will not refuse to do the something that I can do." The Men's Bible Study here at Holy Communion has taught me that there were two things the risen Christ said to his disciples most often, and when I say disciples, I am talking not only about the twelve, but also about you and me. So, in a world full of fear and anger, in a world where King Herod still sometimes reigns, where the Christ child is still in danger of exile from our hearts and minds, I want to leave you with those two things the risen Christ most often says to you and me, his disciples.

BE NOT AFRAID.

and

PEACE BE WITH YOU.

Amen.

THE OVERSOUL

When it was evening on that day, the first day of the week, and the doors of the house where the disciples had met were locked for fear of the Jews, Jesus came and stood among them and said, "Peace be with you." After he said this, he showed them his hands and his side. Then the disciples rejoiced when they saw the Lord. Jesus said to them again, "Peace be with you. As the Father has sent me, so I send you." When he had said this, he breathed on them and said to them, "Receive the Holy Spirit. If you forgive the sins of any, they are forgiven them; if you retain the sins of any, they are retained."

But Thomas (who was called the Twin), one of the twelve, was not with them when Jesus came. So, the other disciples told him, "We have seen the Lord." But he said to them, "Unless I see the mark of the nails in his hands, and put my finger in the mark of the nails and my hand in his side, I will not believe."

A week later his disciples were again in the house, and Thomas was with them. Although the doors were shut, Jesus came and stood among them and said, "Peace be with you." Then he said to Thomas, "Put your finger here and see my hands. Reach out your hand and put it in my side. Do not doubt but believe." Thomas answered him, "My Lord and my God!" Jesus said to him, "Have you believed because you have seen me? Blessed are those who have not seen and yet have come to believe."

Now Jesus did many other signs in the presence of his disciples, which are not written in this book. But these are written so that you may come to believe that Jesus is the Messiah, the Son of God, and that through believing you may have life in his name.

John 20:19-31

Thomas is my favorite disciple. Although some would criticize him for not having faith, I admire him for not blindly accepting the faith of others on hearsay evidence. He wanted his own personal experience of the risen Christ. I respect that. I, too, want a personal experience of the risen Christ. That is what the disciples had that day in the shuttered room.

Prior to that it is amazing how slow and dim-witted the disciples seem in the gospels. They argue about who will be first in the Kingdom of Heaven. Jesus calls Peter Satan. He tells Phillip, " Have I been with you all this time and you still do not know me?" Peter denies Jesus three times, and now Thomas refuses to believe.

But something changes after the resurrection. Something happens to the disciples. They are transformed. They go from total blindness to absolute brilliance in the Book of Acts. These disciples who never seemed to get it, in the gospels, are converting thousands, performing great miracles of healing, even raising people from the dead. They are doing everything that Jesus did. What happened to these guys? What changed?

I believe that what changed was the disciples personal encounter with the risen Christ. They received the Holy Spirit. They were breathed upon by the Christ.

Just as God breathed the breath of life into Adam's nostrils at creation, Jesus breathes the Holy Spirit on his disciples. The gospel lesson for today is a new nativity story. It is the dawn of a new creation. Paul says we have to follow Christ to Jerusalem. We have to be crucified with Christ. We have to be raised with Christ as a **new** creation. You have to be born from above Jesus tells Nicodemus. Paul preaches that we are all members of the mystical body of the risen Christ. The sacrament of the Holy Communion symbolizes the incorporation of the physical elements of Christ into our own bodies. Christ is in us and we are in Christ, Jesus teaches us.

But you and I often isolate ourselves in locked and shuttered rooms out of fear, just like the disciples did. We separate ourselves from others and from God out of fear of rejection, fear of death, fear of illness, fear of the loss of loved ones, fear of financial insecurity, and we doubt, yes, we doubt the resurrection just like Thomas did. But although the doors of our room are shut, Christ can come to us, in our locked room, and he can say to us, "Peace be with you," and he breathes on us, and we receive the Holy Spirit. And it changes us. We are transformed. It is we who are resurrected. We become a mixture of the physical and the spiritual. We become a member of the mystical body of the risen Christ. With the aid of the Holy Spirit, we are restored to God's image and continue in the risen life of Christ, just as all the disciples down through the ages have done.

Ralph Waldo Emerson wrote an essay called the *Oversoul*. I think he was writing about the Holy Spirit. He says:

> "... the Highest dwells within us, ... the sources of nature are in our own minds. ... there is no bar or wall in the soul where we, the effect, cease, and God, the cause, begins. ... There is deep power in which we exist and whose beatitude is accessible to us. ... It comes to the lowly and simple; it comes to whosoever will put off what is foreign and proud; it comes as insight; it comes as serenity and grandeur. The soul's health consists in the fullness of its reception."

Emerson continues:

". . . Within us is the soul of the whole; the wise silence, the universal beauty, to which every part and particle is equally related; the eternal One. When it breaks through our intellect, it is genius; when it breathes through our will, it is virtue; when it flows through our affections, it is love."

So says Emerson. And the risen Christ says to us in our fear-locked and fear-shuttered rooms, "Peace be with you. Receive the Holy Spirit and be transformed for you have seen the Lord." Amen.

NAMASTE

J esus prayed for his disciples, and then he said. "I ask not only on behalf of these, but also on behalf of those who will believe in me through their word, that they may all be one. As you, Father, are in me and I am in you, may they also be in us, so that the world may believe that you have sent me. The glory that you have given me I have given them, so that they may be one, as we are one, I in them and you in me, that they may become completely one, so that the world may know that you have sent me and have loved them even as you have loved me. Father, I desire that those also, whom you have given me, may be with me where I am, to see my glory, which you have given me because you loved me before the foundation of the world.

"Righteous Father, the world does not know you, but I know you; and these know that you have sent me. I made your name known to them, and I will make it known, so that the love with which you have loved me may be in them, and I in them."

John 17:20-26

T oday's lesson is Jesus' Farewell Prayer for his disciples and for those who believe through them. That would mean us. He prays for us. "As you, Father, are in me and I am in you, may they also be in us. . . . that they may be one, as we are one, I in them and you in me, that they may become completely one," It sounds like Russian nesting dolls, doesn't it? You open up the God doll and there's Jesus. Open Jesus and there you and I are. Inside our doll is Jesus again and inside that doll we find God yet again. Christ is in God and God is in Christ. We are in Christ and he is in us.

Richard Rohr writes about the Universal Christ. To Rohr the Universal Christ is the everlasting presence of God's spirit in all creation. To Rohr, creation was the original incarnation of the Spirit. As part of creation, we are part of that original incarnation. We are in creation and creation is in us. We are in the Universal Christ, and it is in us.

Matthew Fox, an Episcopal priest, was the first to articulate this new Creation Theology. To me Creation Theology gives today's lesson clarity. I can now see the Universal Christ in myself. I am in the Christ and this Christ is in me and what's more I can see this Christ in all of creation. I can see it in you. In fact, I see it everywhere I go.

During Lent, Micah Greenstein preached at Calvary. He preached about Rohr's Universal Christ, but, being a Jew, he didn't use the word, Christ. He used a phrase from the Torah. He said we carry the image of God given to us at creation and the image of God in us should respect the image of God in all humans regardless of faith. To Greenstein, the image of God is a universal characteristic we share. A Jew, like Greenstein, calls it the Image of God. A Christian like Fox calls it the Universal Christ.

I have felt this Christ in other places. I practice yoga. As our practice ends, we sit with our hands in prayer. The instructor says, "Thank you for sharing your practice with me," then we bow and say "Namaste," a Sanskrit word meaning, "The divine in me recognizes the divine in you." Or one could say, the Christ in me recognizes the Christ in you or the image of God in me sees the image of

God in you.

I have stumbled on this Christ in even other places. Neil Degras Tyson, an astrophysicist, teaches that after the Big Bang there were two elements in the Universe, helium and hydrogen. They coalesced into stars, and all the other elements of the periodic table were forged inside the furnace of those ancient stars. Eons later they became supernova exploding their new elements into the universe forming more stars, planets, solar systems, and galaxies. Every atom in us was once within those primordial stars. "We are made of stardust!" Tyson says. We have the origins of the Universe within us. We are in the Universe and the Universe is in us. It gives the expression, from dust we came and to dust we must go, an entirely different meaning. We might say from stardust we came and to stardust we must go.

As a straight man when I see a gay man, I say to myself, the Christ in me can see the Christ in him. When we see someone of a different religion, let the image of God in us acknowledges the image of God in them. When people's politics are different from ours, let the divine in us recognize the divine in them. When we encounter other races let us remember that we are made of the same stardust. Seeing the Christ in ourselves and others changes us, connects us, transforms us. Perhaps in this way, as the Gospel says, we can become one, one with one another and one with God.

May the Christ in me see the Christ in you. May the Image of God in me acknowledge the Image of God in you. May the divine in me recognize the divine in you. In this way, may we become one, one with the Father, one with the Christ, and one with each other.

Namaste.

CONCLUSION

To me the Bible is spiritual tool or vehicle. I have heard many people whom I admire say, "I am not religious, but I am spiritual." I agree and disagree with those people at the same time. I consider myself both spiritual and religious. Spirituality or the development of a sense of connectedness with the spirit is the goal. To me religion, like the Bible is the tool or vehicle that moves us closer to the goal of spirituality. Meditation on scripture can lead us closer to the Spirit. Repeating verses over and over again looking for a deeper spirituality can make the Bible more pertinent to life in the twenty-first century. I have found that to be true as I read scripture and write my reflections. Everyone should read the gospel assigned to a particular Sunday, meditate on it, repeat it, and write a reflection. There no right or wrong answer on biblical interpretation. Yours are just as good as mine. It can be a deeply moving spiritual exercise to write a five-to-six-minute reflection on the assigned Gospel. You need no training. You don't have to be a priest or a minister. It is a wonderful way to relate to Holy Scripture. It is a vehicle to move us all closer to the sense of connectedness with the Spirit

If you think my reflections are all wrong, you're probably right, and you're probably wrong because there is no right or wrong. The Spirit moves within different people in different ways. There are many roads to Damascus. Just recognize the Christ within you and within others, and let the same mind be within you that was in Christ Jesus.

Be not afraid. Peace be with you.

Made in the USA
Columbia, SC
11 December 2021

50938909R00057